North Gate, Launceston Castle

THE CASTLES OF
DEVON AND CORNWALL

AND FORTS OF THE SCILLY ISLES

Mike Salter

FOLLY PUBLICATIONS

ACKNOWLEDGEMENTS

The photographs in this book were taken by the author between 1978 and 1998. He also prepared the map and the plans. The old prints and old postcards are reproduced from originals in his collection. Most of the plans are on scales of 1:400 and 1:800, although there are some site plans at 1:2000. Thanks are due to Max Barfield, John Lowe and Andrea Kirkby for help with transport during field trips and to my mother Marjorie Salter who checked through the proofs.

AUTHOR'S NOTES

This series of books (see full list inside the back cover) is intended as portable field guides giving as much information and illustrative material as possible in volumes of modest size, weight and price. Quite a lot of information is given on lesser known buildings. The aim in all the castle books has been to mention, where the information is known to the author, owners or custodians of buildings who erected or altered parts of them, and those who were the first or last of a line to hold an estate, an important office, or a title. Those in occupation at the time of dramatic events such as sieges are also sometimes named. Other owners and occupants whose lives had little effect on the condition or usage of the buildings are generally not mentioned, nor are 19th and 20th century events or ghost stories, myths or legends.

The books are intended to be used in conjunction with the Ordnance Survey 1:50,000 scale maps. Grid references are given in the gazetteers together with a coding system indicating which buildings can be visited or easily seen by the public from adjacent public open spaces which is explained on page 104. One or two grid references for buildings that have left no remains are only approximate.

The books in this series commonly use the pre 1974 county names and boundaries. None of the sites described in this book have been affected by later changes, despite some alterations to the boundary between Devon and Cornwall.

Each level of a building is called a storey in this book, the basement being the first storey with its floor near courtyard level unless specifically mentioned as otherwise.

Measurements given in the text and scales on the plans are metric. Although the buildings were designed using feet and inches the metric scales are much easier and were used for all fieldwork. They are also the standard unit of measurement amongst academics working on historic buildings and ancient sites. For those who feel a need to make a conversion 3 metres is almost 10 feet. Unless specifically mentioned as otherwise all dimensions are external at or near ground level, but above the plinth if there is one. On the plans the original work is shown black, post-1800 work is stippled and alterations or additions of intermediate periods are hatched.

ABOUT THE AUTHOR

Mike Salter is 45 and has been a professional writer and publisher since he went on the Government Enterprise Allowance Scheme for unemployed people in 1988. He is particularly interested in the planning and layout of medieval buildings and has a huge collection of plans of churches and castles he has measured during tours (mostly by bicycle and motorcycle) throughout all parts of the British Isles since 1968. Wolverhampton bord and bred, Mike now lives in an old cottage beside the Malvern Hills. His other interests include walking, maps, railways, board games, morris dancing, playing percussion instruments and calling dances with a folk group.

Copyright 1999 Mike Salter. First published April 1999.
Folly Publications, Folly Cottage, 151 West Malvern Rd, Malvern, Worcs, WR144AY.
Printed by Aspect Design, 89 Newtown Rd, Malvern, Worcs, WR14 2PD

Domestic apartments at Restormel Castle

CONTENTS

INTRODUCTION

Defensible residences of the type known to the Normans as castles were introduced to Devon and Cornwall in the years after 1068, when William I (The Conqueror) besieged and captured the city of Exeter and built a castle within one corner of the Roman defences. Estates were then granted to Norman lords in return for specified periods of military service. The Norman lords or barons then in turn gave units of land called manors to their knights, again in return for military service. This system being known as feudalism. This thin veneer of land-owning Normans consolidated their fragile hold on the land by constructing castles as residences, strongholds and status symbols. The Domesday book of 1086 records several baronial castles as having been erected by then. William I's half brother Robert, Count of Mortain in France had been made Earl of Cornwall with control over 247 manors there. His principal seat was at Launceston (then called Dunhived), but he had a second castle at Trematon, the two being positioned to command the principal access routes into Cornwall. Baldwin de Brionne, Sheriff of Devon, had his seat at Okehampton, whilst a Breton named Judhael had castles at Barnstaple and Totnes, taking his surname from the latter. The castle at Plympton is thought to have been built by the de Redvers family in the 1090s and that at Restormel is assumed to have been built c1100 by Baldwin, Fitz Turstin, son of the Turstin noted in Domesday Book as Sheriff of Cornwall. There are also many other lesser castle sites probably mostly erected either during the reign of Henry I (1100-35) or during the troubled reign of King Stephen (1135-54).

All of the castles named above now have later stonework upon their 11th century earthworks. The royal castle at Exeter has a fine gatehouse probably no later than c1070, foundations remain of another of c1100-20 at Restormel, and parts remain of a modest two storey tower keep at Okehampton. Otherwise the 11th century castles were built of earth and wood, following the pattern for castles elsewhere in England and Wales until castles with stone curtain walls became the norm in the late 12th and 13th centuries. Masons must have been in short supply compared with carpenters and labourers. Evidence of this are the triangular headed upper windows of the gatehouse at Exeter, suggesting it was actually built by Saxon craftsmen as Norman masons never built such features. Restormel originally had a high banked circular enclosure of the type known to castle experts as a ringwork. The inner ward at Exeter could also be classed as a ringwork, although it is larger and square in plan. It is probably no coincidence that these sites each have remains of an early stone gatehouse since the entrances of such enclosures would be easily the weakest point.

Motte at Plympton

The motte at Bampton

The other castles are of a different type with a high mound or motte originally surmounted by the lord's house or tower with a small palisaded court around it, access being by a long timber ramp or steps capable of being easily defended from the summit, especially if there was a drawbridge at the top. Both mottes and ringworks were usually accompanied by a bailey or court surrounded by a rampart, palisade and ditch, and containing a hall, chapel, workshops, and stores. The motte or ringwork formed the citadel or last refuge if the weaker defences of the bailey should succumb to an attack. Some mottes are entirely man-made but those of the more important castles of Devon and Cornwall tend to be natural ridges or hummocks heightened, steepened and generally made into a more regular pudding type shape. The unusual rectangular mound at Okehampton is probably mostly natural, especially since it bears a stone tower not much (if at all) younger than its adoption as a castle mound. The mound at Totnes contains footings of modest width probably for a timber tower. Buried in woods at Wembworthy in Devon is the curious feature of a ringwork and bailey with a second similar but more elongated site on a cliff-edge close by.

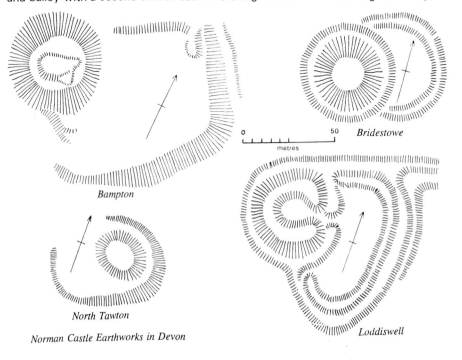

Bridestowe

0 ⊢⊢⊢⊢⊢⊢ 50
metres

Bampton

North Tawton

Loddiswell

Norman Castle Earthworks in Devon

As happened elsewhere in England and Wales the timber buildings and defences of the major castles were gradually replaced by structures of mortared stone. Unfortunately records of construction work on castles in Devon and Cornwall are almost unknown until the 14th century. When a small palisaded court on the motte was rebuilt in stone the result is what modern experts call a shell keep. Devon and Cornwall are noted for having keeps of this type since there are few major castles not having mottes, and although Compton and Berry Pomeroy are well known the other stronghouses are too altered or fragmentary to be well known nationally. The shell keeps at Launceston and Trematon are probably of c1160-1200, the latter being exceptionally complete and unaltered. Probably of the same period is the more fragmentary shell keep at Plympton with evidence of beams buried within the masonry to strengthen it. Nothing now remains visible of other 12th century shell keeps at Barnstaple and Truro. The rather larger shell wall which replaced the inner part of the rampart of the ringwork at Restormel was once thought to be of c1200 but is now generally accepted as late 13th century. Restormel is often quoted as being a typical shell keep, but in fact it is quite unusual in several ways. Because it has never been open to the public the much more typical shell keep at Trematon has tended to be overlooked in favour of Restormel and another well-preserved structure also long accessible to the public, the keep at Totnes, a 14th century rebuilding of of a 12th or 13th century shell keep.

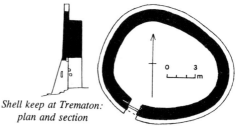

Shell keep at Trematon:
plan and section

The shell keep at Trematon   The gatehouse at Trematon

The bailey curtain wall at Trematon

Of other probable 12th century structures amongst the castles of Devon and Cornwall there is surprisingly little to report. Footings have been revealed of a thick early curtain wall on the north side of the bailey at Okehampton. At Launceston is part of an early gatehouse plus the base of a mural tower which was perhaps of wood since the the bailey then only still had a palisade. Exeter has more impressive remains for most of the circuit of the early stone curtain wall of the inner ward still remains together with one square corner tower. Two sides lie above and may incorporate parts of the Roman city walls and the rest probably existed by 1136, when the castle, then held by Baldwin de Redvers, defied King Stephen for three months. De Redvers other castle at Plympton was captured and burnt during this campaign in which the castle at Bampton also played a part. The other important relic is the basement of a square tower keep, possibly the prison built in 1195 by Richard I to serve the Stannary Courts of the tin miners of Dartmoor. The superstructure built upon this basement must be 13th century work. The only work in the castles of Devon and Cornwall which can be assigned to King John's reign (1199-1216) is the stump of a polygonal tower with pilaster buttreses of c1210 at Exeter, where the outer ward may then have been provided with stone walls.

Keep at Lydford

In 1227 Henry III created a new earldom of Cornwall for his brother Richard. This earl did not spend much of his time in Cornwall, especially in his later years when his interests lay on the continent with his election as King of the Romans in 1257, but c1230-45 he was responsible for major works at Launceston and Tintagel. Richard is thought to have fortified the latter site with two enclosures defending a causeway access to a headland (now an island) as part of the resurrection of the Arthurian legends then popular. There is in fact no definite evidence of a connection between King Arthur and Tintagel although the headland has ruins of dwellings of about his period. The castle is more remarkable for its location than for its architecture, the design being conservative for its date. At Launceston the bailey was finally walled in stone, given new gatehouses and internal buildings which long remained in use for the administration of juctice within Cornwall. More dramatic were developments on the motte, a two storey round tower being raised within the older shell keep and a mantlet built around the base of it, giving three embattled lines of defence, the whole being approached by a flight of steps with a gatehouse at the bottom. The new keep seems to have functioned as a place for state ceremony rather than as a lordly residence, since the earl had a suite of chambers in the bailey. An old illustration suggests a possible similar tower within the shell keep at Plympton.

Trematon has a fine rectangular gatehouse of the 1250s or 60s and the north gatehouse at Launceston is of the 1270s or 80s. Little remains of the original keep and bailey built by Henry III on Lundy in the 1240s. The shell wall and the contemporary suite of curved chambers fitted within it at Restormel are thought to be the work of Richard's son Edmund, Earl of Cornwall from 1272 to 1299. Restormel was not a particularly strong fortress, being more important as a residence and administrative centre. The domestic buildings are unusually complete and unaltered, the only real rival set being at Okehampton. Most of what remains at Okehampton was built by Hugh Courtenay between 1297 and 1335, when Edward III finally granted him the earldom of Devon he long aspired to. The tower on the motte was doubled in length and the long narrow bailey extending from it to a square gatehouse with a long barbican beyond was almost filled with domestic buildings. As at Restormel the domestic arangements were sumptuous and up-to-date whilst the defences only gave basic security with no provision for flanking fire on the exposed north side. Flanking towers are uncommon in Devon and Cornwall and the bailey wall at Totnes, rebuilt along with the keep in the early 14th century, never had any.

Upper ward at Tintagel

The domestic buildings at Okehampton

By the 14th century the fashion for new castles was a rectangular court with corner towers, usually round in southern England, and a twin-towered gatehouse. The Courtenays other seat at Tiverton dating from the late 13th and early 14th century conformed more to this plan, though the layout was far from regular with corner towers of differing shapes and sizes and a rectangular gatehouse in the middle of one side. Devon contained three late 14th century castles with quadrangular courts. Hardly anything now remains at Lanihorne but there is a lofty section of straight curtain walling and one very ruined round corner tower at Dartmouth. At Hemyock are fragments of several round towers set at the corners and on either side of a gateway, plus remains of a wet moat. The towers are thinly walled and do not appear to have been habitable so we can only conclude they were more for show than for series defence. Dartmouth had a genuine military purpose, being built by the townsfolk to defend the harbour mouth against French raiders, but Lanihorne was probably another status symbol castellated residence rather than a serious fortress. Some work was done on the domestic buildings at Tintagel in the mid 14th century but by then the site had little importance. The only 15th century building of note apart from the coastal artillery forts of the 1480s is the curious and tiny double towered structure perched on a granite crag at Carn Brea.

1st STOREY

2nd STOREY

0   3
m

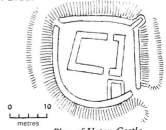

0   10
metres

Trematon: plans of gatehouse

Plan of Upton Castle

The small tower of c1300-10 at Gidleigh is the earliest of a series of stronghouses in Devon offering security against burglary or minor raiding but not designed to withstand a full-scale attack. Another of this series is Powderham, a secondary Courtenay seat of the 1390s with a long narrow main block with one square corner corner flanking the main frontage facing the approach to the promontory site. The layout vaguely recalls the contemporary castle of Doune in Perthshire but was nothing like as strong since the Buck brothers engraving shows us that the embattled walls of the court behind the domestic block were thin and low, perhaps even without a wall-walk. At Doune the lord had his apartments in a mighty tower over the gateway beside the hall whereas the gatehouse at Powderham was a small tower at the opposite end of the court facing towards the sea. Colcombe, often described as a fortified manor house, may not have had defences.. The Poles' seat at Shute Barton was three storeys high and embattled but with thin walls with big windows at ground level. Bickleigh has an impressive gatehouse block on one site of a moated court. The tower added c1460 to Place House, Fowey, was probably mostly a status symbol.

Two slightly later buildings dating from the c1485-95 and c1500-20 respectively, Berry Pomeroy and Compton, are better preserved, more impressive, and more capable of resisting raiders. Berry Pomeroy has a strong promontory site with a large 16th century mansion closed off by a late medieval curtain wall with a gatehouse at one end and a flanking tower at the other, both parts being equipped with ports for discharging firearms. At Compton a 14th century manor house with 15th century added wings lying in a hollow ended up with apartments around small courts on either side of the hall with a set of six square lofty flanking towers. The towers have no battlements and the box-machicolations, a rare feature in England, are perhaps largely for show since they are all massed on the approach side. However, gunloops in the towers command the narrow and high-walled outer court, making this confined space an effective killing ground for attackers trapped within it.

In the medieval period castle walls of rubble were often limewashed outside making them look very different from the way they appear today. Dressed stoned around windows and doorways would be left uncovered. Domestic rooms would have had whitewashed rooms decorated with murals of biblical, historical or heroic scenes mostly painted in red, yellow and black. Wall hangings decorated with the same themes or heraldry gradually became more common from the 14th century onwards. Although used in churches, glass was expensive and uncommon in secular buildings before the 15th century, so windows were originally closed with wooden shutters. As a result rooms were dark when the weather was too cold or wet for them to be opened for light and ventilation. Large openings in the outer walls sometimes had iron bars or projecting grilles even if high above ground level, as at Compton. Living rooms usually has fireplaces although some halls had central hearths with the smoke escaping through louvres in the roof. Latrines are common and indicate which rooms were for living, working or sleeping in, rather than just storage space.

Furnishings were sparse up until the 15th century although the embrasures of upper storey windows sometimes have built-in stone seats. Lords with several castles tended to circulate around them, administering their manorial courts and consuming agricultural produce on the spot. Seats belonging to great lords could be left almost empty when they were not in residence. For most of their lives places like Tintagel gradually crumbled away with only a skeleton staff in residence to administer the estates. Servants travelled with lords and sometimes also portable furnishings such as rugs, wall hangings, cooking vessels and bedding, all kept in wooden chests. The lord and his immediately family plus honoured guests and the senior household officials would enjoy a fair degree of privacy, having their own rooms. Servants and retainers enjoyed less comfort and privacy, sharing of beds and communal sleeping in hall and warm places of work like the kitchens and stables being common.

From the late 14th century onwards the fine harbours amongst the estuaries of the south coast of Devon and Cornwall were at risk from French raids in reprisal for attacks by English seafarers. The development of cannon necessitated the construction of new defences at the mouth of the River Dart in the 1480s. A chain was stretched across the river between two towers at the waters edge equipped with gunports. Henry VIII feared a foreign invasion after he took the English church away from papal control in the mid 1530s and a new series of forts were built along the whole of the south coast, some of them being intended to be defensible against an attack by land as well as sea. The estuary of the river Fal was commanded by forts built on either side at Pendennis and St Mawes. Both have low round central keeps containing accommodation for gunners whose cannon were mounted at Pendennis on a circular surrounding chemise, whilst St Mawes has three interlocked round bastions giving a trilobed plan. Both forts were supplimented by blockhouses at the water's edge for cannon of that period could not easily be angled down to command a river mouth from the cliffs above. For this same reason a small fort of the 1550s called King Charles Castle on Tresco in the Scilly Isles was superseded a century later by a round tower called Cromwell's Castle on the shore below. Another round tower of the 1650s stood on Mount Batten Point opposite Plymouth. At Fowey there was a fort on the cliff with cannon firing out to sea and then blockhouses on each shore of the eastuary with a chain stretched between them, and there are remains of another fort at Salcome. Also of this period are many blockhouses around Plymouth and the tower added to a previously undefended house at Pengerswick, close to the south coast. Gunports also appear in non-military buildings such as the gatehouse of Tavistock Abbey and in a guard room by a gateway at Cotehele manor house.

St Mawes Castle   *Pendennis Castle*

King Charles' Castle, Tresco, Isles of Scilly

Queen Elizabeth I also spent much of her reign (1558-1603) fearing a foreign invasion with the intention of replacing her with a Catholic monarch. The Armada of 1588 proved her fears were justified. He father's forts were all maintained and some of them improved, the upper fort at Pendennis being surrounded by a large bastioned fort in the 1590s. The unfinished fort of Harry's Walls probably of 1551-4 on St Mary's in the Scilly Isles was a square with arrow-head shaped corner bastions. It was superseded in 1593 by Star Castle, an eight-pointed star-shaped block closely surrounded by a thick rampart of the same shape. It lies within a large later enciente defending an entire headland and having bastions of varying size and shape.

The castle and city of Exeter withstood attacks during the rebellions of 1497 and 1549, although Trematon was captured during the latter conflict. By the time Civil War broke out between King Charles I and Parliament in 1642 the medieval castles of Devon and Cornwall were mostly in a sorry state of decay. The castle and walled town of Launceston changed hands several times during the 1640s. Both there and at Okehampton and Exeter only one or two chambers seem to have been sufficiently in repair to be used by the late 17th century. Restormel also played a part in the conflict. The Royalist commander of St Mawes decided the fort was untenable against a serious landward bombardment and surrendered but Pendennis proved one of the hardest places for the victorious Parlimentarians to capture.

Charles II had a huge new bastioned citadel built at Plymouth in the 1660s. It and the forts at St Mawes, Pendennis and Dartmouth were kept in repair right through to modern times, additional batteries with more modern weapons being added when thought necessary. Kingswear also survives intact but is not open to the public (by English Heritage) like the others, being a holiday home. Of the other places described in this book Place House at Fowey, the tower at Pengerswick and Bickleigh are still private residences, as is Trematon. The defences there remained intact until c1809 part of the bailey wall was demolished to allow a seaward view from a new house built within it, St Michael's Mount has remained a residence and is now a National Trust property, and Carn Brea has been recently extended to accommodate a restaurant. Tiverton still remains a residence, parts being ruined since slighting in 1647 and other parts having been altered and extended over the years. The ruins at Hemyock surround a farmhouse of various periods. Compton is mostly intact and cared for by the National Trust, whilst Berry Pomeroy, Launceston, Okehampton, Restormel, Tintagel and Totnes are ruins cared for by English Heritage. On the Scilly Isles Star Castle is a hotel and the other ruined forts and battery sites are freely accessible. Also freely accessible are the mottes at Bampton, Barnstaple and Plympton, the ruins of the fort at Salcome (at low tide), the blockhouses and forts at Fowey, Polruan and Little Dennis and several of the blockhouses around Plymouth.

FORTIFICATIONS OF THE SCILLY ISLES

Not much is known of the medieval occupation of the Scilly Islands and little remains of Ennor, the only stronghold of that period. Of far greater interest is the series of blockhouses and artillery forts built during the 16th and 17th centuries. The islands were not included in Henry VIII's coastal defence scheme of 1542 and it was not until one of the Godolphins was made Captain of the Islands under Edward VI in 1549 that the series of forts was begun. Tresco was provided with a blockhouse on the east side and the fort known as King Charles' Castle on the NW, with apparently another blockhouse below it. On St Mary's a fort of the latest type with arrow-head shaped bastions was begun at Harry's Walls but left imcomplete as it was badly sited. In 1570 Queen Elizebeth I leased the Isles of Scilly to Francis Godolphin for 38 years, the rent in 1579 being £20 per annum. By this time the islands were considered vulnerable to an attack by the Spanish and in 1593 work was begun on Star Castle. About ten years later the headland on which it lies was closed off by a rampart, originally of earth but later rebuilt in stone.

The Isles of Scilly were held by the Royalists throughout the Civil War. St Mary's was well fortified with batteries on Peninnis Head, at Carn Morval Point, at Bar Point at Pellow's Redoubt on Toll's Island on the east side, and at two other places between these last two so as to command Crow Sound, whilst the whole of the Hugh peninsular was enclosed by ramparts and ditches. On Tresco a bastioned enclosure was added to King Charles' Castle and a pentagonal fort built on Crown Point at the south end of the island. A battery was also built at the south end of Bryher. Not until 1651 was Parliament able to send a fleet under Admiral Blake to reduce the islands. Blake managed to capture Tresco after landing on the less well fortified east side. He then set up an artillery emplacement later known as Oliver's Battery above and within the older Royalist fort at Crow Point. Although the harbour of St Mary's Pool is 2.5km away his cannon here were able to fire that far, which was enough to induce the Royalists on St Mary's to surrender. The defences were maintained by Parliament and a new artillery tower called Cromwell's Castle built on Tresco to replace an older blockhouse. The Scilly Isles were returned to the Godolphin family at the Restoration of Charles II in 1660 and continued to be leased by them until 1831. The defences of the Hugh peninsular were strengthened between 1715 and 1746 and it became known as The Garrison. The Scilly Isles retain their own system of government under the Crown and have never been part of the county of Cornwall.

King Charles' Castle

Star Castle   *Cromwell's Castle*

ENNOR CASTLE   SV 914102

Within a bend of the road at Old Town on St Mary's is a scrub covered granite knoll with slight traces of retaining walls, suggesting a small polygonal court on the summit, like a shell keep, but here without any obvious signs of an accompanying bailey. It was held by Ranulph de Blanchminster in 1306 on condition he retained a force of 12 men-at-arms to keep the peace on the islands, for which he paid an annual rent of 300 puffins or 6s.8d.

HARRY'S WALLS   SV 910109   F

The Harry referred to in the name must be Henry VIII, but this fort seems to have been that begun in 1551 on the orders of Edward VI's Privy Council, four years after Henry's death. The lower part of the west side only remains of the fort, which seems to have been left incomplete and soon dismantled, although two sakers were mounted upon it in 1554 to command the harbour of St Mary's Pool. What remains corresponds with a plan for a fort in the Scilly Isles preserved at Hatfield House. The plan shows the fort as square with arrow-head shaped bastions of the most up-to-date type on all four corners and the courtyard 25m square within the 6.5m thick walls as containing barrack rooms on all four sides.

Outer gate of The Garrison

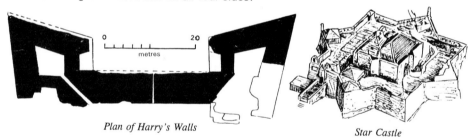

Plan of Harry's Walls

Star Castle

Star Castle

Harry's Walls

STAR CASTLE AND THE GARRISON   SV 899106   H

Francis Godolphin had this fort built uder the supervision of the engineer Robert Adams in 1593, the year that appears over the entrance. A thick rampart with an external batter rising from a rock-cut ditch closely surrounds a low central building, both parts having the unusual plan form of an eight-pointed star. The rampart originally had a blocked-up gunport in each re-entrant angle. The gateway has a portcullis groove and has an 18th century bellcote nearby. The central building contained two levels of barrack rooms over a storage basement. The floor beams are carried on a large central pier in which are two original fireplaces. The original stair was probably also contrived within this pier. The existing stair and some windows are of the 1660s and the rest of the existing openings are later.

Star Castle lies towards the north end of a peninsular known as The Hugh and commanded both the north and south harbours of what is now Hughtown. In the early 1600s Francis Goldophin closed off the whole peninsular with a wall with bastions. By the time of Admiral Blake's invasion an earth rampart with bastions had been erected around the whole of peninsular, the enclosed area being 0.7km long from north to south and 0.5km wide from east to west. Except on the west the enciente was rebuilt in stone between 1715 and 1746 under the supervision of Master Gunner Abraham Tovey, whose initials appear over the gateway towards Hughtown. Grouped close to the gateway are the guard house, barracks, magazine and prison whilst the storehouse and Master Gunner's house lie further west. From this period onwards the Hugh peninsular was known as The Garrison.

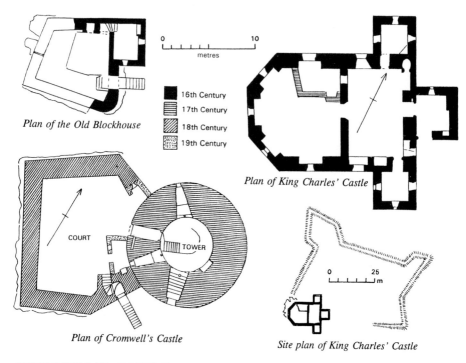

Plan of the Old Blockhouse

■ 16th Century
▦ 17th Century
▨ 18th Century
▒ 19th Century

0   10
metres

Plan of King Charles' Castle

COURT

TOWER

Plan of Cromwell's Castle

0   25
m

Site plan of King Charles' Castle

CROMWELL'S CASTLE   SV 881159   F

In 1651 a small blockhouse of c1550 was replaced by a massive round tower 13.5m in diameter over walls 4m thick and 15m high. Set on a rocky platform by the shore on the NW side of Tresco, this tower allowed the sound between Tresco and Bryher to more directly commanded by cannon than was possible from King Charles' Castle on the hill above in an age before guns that could be easily depressed downwards existed. The original entrance is that on the south side high up, from which steps led down to a living room with two loops and a fireplace. Below was an unlit basement and above a room with a rib vault and a fireplace, dimly lighted by one loop. From this loop a stair led up to a flagged platform. The outer wall here has six gunports with wide external splays and, being still 2m thick, was able to carry a wall-walk and parapet above. A doorway low down on the west side gave access to a battery of six guns replaced c1740 by the existing pentangular platform with its own access from the shore on the SE side. The platform has a guard room with a fireplace near the entrance, and there is a latrine on the north beside the round tower outer wall.

GRIMSBY: OLD BLOCKHOUSE   SV 897155   F

On a headland 0.5km east of Grimsby parish church on Tresco is a quadrangular blockhouse described in a Parliamentary survey of 1652 as Dover Fort. It consisted of an open platform 7m across enclosed by a wall 1.1m thick, now reduced on the NE and NW sides which must have each one contained at least two gunports. The entrance on the SW reached by steps is flanked by a thinly walled room added later with two small windows and a fireplace. Close by the steps down to the room from the platform is an ammunition locker with a stone corbelled roof.

The Old Blockhouse

Cromwell's Castle

KING CHARLES' CASTLE   SV 882161   F

On a headland near the NW end of Tresco, overlooking the north end of the sound between Tresco and Bryher is a fort begun c1550 and equipped with artillery in 1554. It is a rectangular building 18.8m long by 12.2m long over walls 1.5m thick. The western corners are cambered off, this end being an open emplacement for five cannon firing through wide mouthed gunports looking north, NE, west, SW and south. The eastern part formed accommodation for the gunners and has fireplaces on the south and east sides, the latter having an oven in the NE corner. The doorway in the east wall has a drawbar slot and was protected by a porch, now much ruined, with its outer entrance facing south. Similar wings 5m wide project 4m from the eastern end of the north and south walls, providing small private rooms. Another private room was later closed off within the NE corner of the open emplacement, one cannon being removed. The ruin lies in the SW corner of a worn-down earth-banked enclosure 120m by 150m dating from the Civil War period. There is a sharp-pointed bastion at the NW corner and and a demi-bastion at the NE corner.

King Charles' Castle

GAZETTEER OF CASTLES IN CORNWALL

BINHAMY   SS 219058

An overgrown square platform 60m by 50m surrounded by an almost dry moat 2m deep and 10m wide near Stratton is all that remains of a fortified manor house, for which Ralph de Blanchminster was granted a licence to crenellate by Edward III in 1335. It is mentioned as the seat of Sir John Colshill by William of Worcester in 1478, whilst Norden later calls it "a ruyned auntient seate of the Grenviles".

BOSCASTLE   SX 099909

Slight traces remain on the end of a ridge called Jordans not far from Tintagel. The castle built by the de Bottreaux family in the reign of Henry II. It is mentioned as a "place" in 1297.

BOSSINNEY   SX 066888   V

A damaged ringwork about 30m across with a high rampart and ditch on the NW side and traces of a bailey 60m wide extending 100m to the SW may be the site of a castle built by Earl Robert de Mortain in the late 11th century. It may have been abandoned in favour of the new castle at Tintagel in the 13th century.

CARDINHAM   SX 127681

Richard Fitz-Turold, Steward to Earl Robert de Mortain, is thought to have had his seat here above a stream 0.5km south of the church, where there are worn down earthworks of a ringwork 50m by 35m within an oval bailey 90m wide extending 80m towards the approach from the SE. The ringwork looks as if it once contained stone buildings, the Cardinham family being occupants of the site in the 14th century.

0   50
L___I___I___I___Im

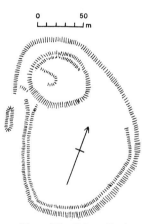

Plan of Cardinham Castle

Plan of Carn Brea Castle

0   3
L___I___Im

Carn Brea Castle

Ringwork at Bossiney

Carn Brea Castle

CARN BREA   SW 687406   H

This is one of the strangest medieval castellated structures in England. On a boss of granite within the ramparts of an Iron Age hillfort are two turrets both about 3m wide externally and 2m wide internally with a length of about 6m and connected by a narrow passage. An entrance reached by a flight of steps up the west side of the rock leads into the SW corner of the NE turret, which has a wedge shaped north end. This part may be later. The whole structure has the character of an 18th century folly or gazebo but older features survive and the SW part at least must be the "Turris Castelli" held by Sir John Basset when William of Worcester visited Cornwall c1478. Leland also mentions it and says "There was sumtyme a park now defacid". The castle was perhaps a status symbol or beacon since it was visible throughout the Bassets' manor of Tehidy, but it may originally have been an oratory dedicated to St Michael, a common dedication for hilltop chapels. There are several 17th and 18th century references to the foot (i.e below) St Michael, and there is a record of Bishop Lacy of Exeter granting William and Margaret Basset a licence for "Chapels or oratories at Tehidy and Carnbre". It also recalls the chapel perched on a granite outcrop at Roche. In 1330 Edward III granted William Basset a licence for the crenellation of the manor house at Tehidy but no relics of that period survive there.

By the early 18th century the castle of Carn Brea was ruinous but the Bassets had restored and possibly enlarged the building by the 1750s. In the late 19th century there was another restoration when a south wing was added and the building leased to a tenant who was bound under the agreement to display a light towards Tehidy to the NW, which thus served as a landmark for sailors in the Bristol Channel. The tenants admitted "visitors to the roof of the castle at a penny per head". Two new windows were inserted in the east turret in 1936 and a garden formed on a shelf below the NW side. When in 1944 the letting was advertised there were said to be five rooms with a water supply from a well. In the 1950s the empty building was damaged by vandals but was repaired and re-let after being sold to a Mrs Hill in 1957. In the 1970s the castle was again restored after a period of dereliction, the access to a cellar formed in a cleft in the rock being re-opened. Close to this is a latrine shaft, clearly a medieval feature. In 1979 a new wing was added on the south side containing kitchens and the castle has since served as a restaurant.

CASTLE DORE   SX 104548   F

This earthwork has a commanding position beside the Fowey to Lostwithiel road. The 3m high rampart rising above a ditch 1.5m deep to enclose a court 70m across dates from the Iron Age. King Mark of Cornwall is said to have had a timber hall here in the 6th century. There is no evidence of medieval occupation of the site and it is mentioned here on account of it being occupied in 1644 by a Parliamentary army under the Earl of Essex. After a desperate fight lasting a whole day they were forced to surrender to the Royalists, although Essex himself managed to escape.

FOWEY   SX 125517, 118509, & 121513

Ince Castle

According to Leland the merchant Thomas Treffry added a fine embattled tower to his mansion of Place House on a shelf of land above the parish church after a French attack in 1457. He was absent at the time but his wife, aided by her servants, managed to ward off the raiders. In the church is a fine tomb with effigies of three men probably Thomas's grandsons, attainted by Richard III but restored by Henry VII. Their father John was county sheriff in 1482. Another Thomas Treffry was exiled for his opposition to the marriage of Queen Mary with Philip of Spain. A tower at the west end stands on the site of the 15th century one, which collapsed in the 18th century. The rest of the house is a mixture of work of the Tudor, Georgian and Victorian periods.

On a rock overlooking the mouth of the Fowey estuary is a D-shaped blockhouse for four cannon which Henry VIII had erected in 1542. Known as St Catherine's Castle, the blockhouse measures about 7.5m across each way over walls 1.3m thick. The natural rock-face forms the base of the straight NW wall. Two gunloops face east and SE and the pointed-headed doorway and other opening face NE where there is a thinner walled later building. Also on that side, at a lower level, are two gun emplacements of much later date. There is free access to this site at anytime.

Set by the shore against the cliffs half way between the other two sites are remains of a rectangular 15th or 16th century blockhouse, the west wall being almost complete but the seaward walls much ruined. A chain was stretched from here across the mouth of the estuary to a tower at Polruan opposite.

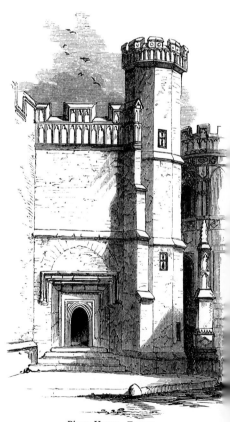

Place House, Fowey

Old postcard of St Catherine's Castle, Fowey

HELSTON

A bowling green in a public park is said to lie on the site of a castle built probably by Edmund, Earl of Cornwall in the late 13th century. It seems to have gone by 1478 but is mentioned by Leland c1540.

INCE   SX 401565

This domestic-looking brick building with granite dressings and bold cornices lies on a promontory beside the St Germans River. It seems to have been erected c1640-2 by Sir Henry Killigrew, who died in 1646 of wounds received during the Royalist evacuation of Plymouth, leaving Ince to his mistress Jane and her son Henry Hill. About that time the castle surrendered to Colonel Weldon after a siege lasting a few hours and was found to contain 5 barrels of powder, 90 muskets and 4 minions (small cannon). It was then sold to the Truro merchant Edward Nesworthy. A wing at the back was added in the 1920s and it remains a private residence of Viscount Boyd of Merton. The main block is a square of two storeys with square pyramidal-roofed, four storey corner towers, some of which contain spiral staircases.

KILKHAMPTON   SS 243116   F

Although of modest size this earthwork is quite strong and commands a considerable view. It consists of a motte with two baileys up to 30m wide and 65m long in total extending towards the approach from the east. The rampart dividing the baileys is 4m high on the east side. The motte rises 6m above the deep ditch surrounding the whole site to a D-shaped summit 20m long by 12m wide. This castle is thought to have been erected by Robert of Gloucester c1140 in support of the Empress Matilda against King Stephen. It was probably destroyed during Henry II's reign by Reginald, Earl of Cornwall.

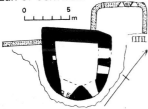

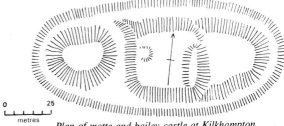

St Catherine's Castle: plan   metres   *Plan of motte and bailey castle at Kilkhampton*

LANIHORNE SW 895420 V

A thin and low stub of a wall towards the creek of the Ruan River is the only possible relic of the seat of Sir John Lercedekne (or Archdekne) for the crenellation of which Edward III granted a licence in 1335. Leland describes it as "decaying, for lack of coverture", and says it was "sumtyme a castel of 8 tours" There are said to have been two walled courts. In 1730 Tonkin refers to one round tower as being large and "at least fifty feet in height". Several other towers also survived until the place was dismantled c1718 by a Mr Grant, the materials being used to build houses for a new port called Ruan Lanihorne for vessels of up to 100 tons. The port is now silted up.

LAUNCESTON SX 331847 E

The earldom of Conwall was granted by William the Conqueror to his half brother Robert de Mortain. He made Launceston, or Dunhevet, as it was then called, the administrative centre of his estates and he is recorded in Domesday Book as having a castle here. The earldom was held from the 1140s until 1175 by Reginald, an illegitimate son of Henry I, who perhaps built the shell keep on the motte, and then reverted to the Crown. King Stephen granted a pension to the castle chaplain and about that time the castle was under the command of Halveth Malyverer. It was commanded by Walter Reynell in 1189. Richard I granted the castle to John, Count of Mortain but it reverted to the Crown after Prince's John's rebellion in 1191. Henry III granted the castle to his brother Richard, created Earl of Cornwall in 1227. He remodelled the castle, adding a round tower within the shell wall, building a new curtain wall round the bailey, and probably new domestic buildings. The castle reverted to the Crown when his son Edmund died childless in 1299.

Launceston: the gateway at the approach to the keep

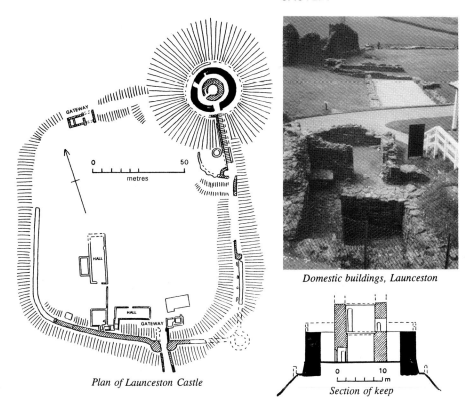

Domestic buildings, Launceston

Plan of Launceston Castle

Section of keep

In 1337 the castle was surveyed on behalf of Edward III's young son Edward, created Duke of Cornwall that year. The survey refers to the curtain walls as ruinous and needing repair, and to "a certain hall with two cellars which require to be newly-roofed, one sufficient kitchen annexed to the same hall, a small upstairs hall which is called the Earl's Chamber; with a chamber and a small chapel, the walls of which are of timber and plank, and the timber thereof almost disjointed; and two chambers above the two gates, sufficiently covered with lead; one old and feeble small hall with a chamber and a cellar, convenient for the Constable, and one little kitchen annexed. There is also one chapel in good order, except the windows which are weak; two stables sufficient for ten horses; one gaol, badly and weakly covered with lead; and one other prison, called the Larder, weak and almost useless; and one passage leading from the castle even to the high tower recently covered with lead, nevertheless the steps of the same are deficient; and there are in the same tower two chambers of which the doors and windows are of no value; and the tower has two mantlet walls of which one part by estimation three perches has fallen to the ground...". The survey also refers to a park containing fifteen deer. It is evident that the keep was then little used. Of the three halls in the bailey the main hall was used "for syses and sessions" as Leland put it in 1539. It was repaired in 1341-3 along with the "mantlet" of the keep, and long remained in use, Launceston retaining the functions of the county town until 1840. The earl's hall was little used since they were mostly absentee lords, whilst the small hall for the constable and the chapel seem to have survived until the 17th century.

South Gateway at Launceston

The keep at Launceston

Launceston:
plans of keep

The later history of the castle as part of the duchy usually held by the eldest son of the monarch is one of minimal maintenance until the early 16th century and then abandonment apart from the buildings needed to hold the assize courts. In 1353 the townsfolk were ordered to desist from allowing their pigs from tramping down the moat, the consequent ground movement endangering the foundations of the curtain walls, which suggests they were rather poorly built in the first place. In 1361 the bridge in front of the south gate was much in need of repair. Repairs were executed in 1382-3 and substantial work was executed in 1406-9, several roofs, doorways and windows being replaced, ivy cut away from the walls, and a new section of embattled parapet constructed; unfortunately we do not know whereabouts in the castle this was. Edward IV had further repairs carried out in 1461-4. The town and castle were held for King Charles during the Civil War, finally surrendering to Fairfax in February 1646. In April that year there is reference to "4 days work" on repairing the defences of the castle and town walls. In 1650 a report describes the hall and chapel "quite level with the ground", the prison had been recently stripped of its lead roof and the only habitable part seems to have been two rooms behind the south gatehouse. In later years the castle site was leased by the town council and laid out as a public park. An Air Ministry office was set up within the bailey during the 1939-45 war and in 1951 the castle passed into the guardianship of the Ministry of Works, now succeeded by English Heritage.

The castle has a rectangular bailey about 120m from north to south by 100m from east to west. The keep and motte lie in the NE corner and there are gateways in the middle of each of the north and south sides. Not much remains of the curtain wall except for a 50m long section on the south side west of the south gate, and foundations on the east and west sides. In three places there was slight evidence of small stone towers of the 12th century, although the curtain itself appears to be of c1227-40. The south gate is mostly also of that period, but the thin walls enclosing a barbican in front of it are later. The arch was closed by a portcullis and is flanked by solid round towers about 5m in diameter. Nothing now remains of the older inner parts of the gatehouse in which were chambers used by the constable. The north gate is probably of c1275-90 and has a passage with a ribbed vault. The outer arch is rebuilt but the triple-chamfered inner arch retains a portcullis groove. West of the gateway is a rectangular room called the Doomsdale Tower. In the bailey lie the recently exposed footings of two groups of halls with their ancilliary chambers.

A long flight of steps leads up beside the east curtain to the keep. The steps were roofed over and were protected by a gate at the bottom with a D-shaped tower on the west side. There were once steps leading up to a room over the gate and the curtain wall-walk. A terrace with a well adjoins the west side of the steps. The entrance arch of the shell wall is now no more than a ragged hole. Originally the wall projected here and had a portcullis groove. The shell wall is up to 3.8m thick above a battered base with a string course and encloses what was originally a court 17.8m by 15.8m. This keep is more massive than others of its type and the fact that the motte has been able to bear its weight suggests the foundations may go down to natural soil not far below the present motte surface. The wall contained a chamber, now very ruined, on the NW and two stairs to the wall-walk, one of them ascending from the entrance. A round tower 12m in diameter over walls 3m. thick was later built in the middle of the court, the space between the tower and shell then being roofed over. The tower, now leaning 1m out of vertical, has an entrance facing west but no other features at ground level. A stair curves round in the wall thickness from the entrance to a window embrasure of the room above, and then continues up to the wall-head. This upper room also has another window opposite and a fireplace. Altogether this keep was a formidable strongpoint but it scarcely formed an adequate lordly residence, hence hall and chambers reserved for the lord in the bailey. It seems that the tower upper room was a state chamber only intended for occasional use with much pomp and show. In later years the tower seems to have been used only as a prison. Not only did the tower and shell both have embattled parapets but there was a lower outer retaining mantlet wall with a parapet outside the shell. It was probably this wall that required rebuilding in 1337. When complete this triple array of battlements must have looked most impressive, a stunning symbol of lordly power.

Of the 13th century town walls a section remains on the south side plus a square gatehouse with two much altered upper storeys with mullioned windows.

MOUNT EDGCUMBE   SX 456532   O

Close to the shore, but now divided from it by a 19th century terrace below the house of Mount Edgcumbe, is a well preserved blockhouse 6.3m square, probably dating from 1542. An entrance with a pointed arch faces towards the house. There are slots for drawbars, the entrance is recessed so that it could be covered by a machicolation behind the outer lintel, and it is also covered by a pistol loop opening off a straight stair leading up the battlements. The single room is covered by a concrete roof and has double-splayed gunports facing east and south.

SECTION

Mount Edgcumbe

PENDENNIS   SW 824317   E

The headland occupied by this castle is a splendid site for a fortification and the dennis or dinas part of the name suggests it was used as such in prehistoric times. In 1540 Henry VIII ordered the erection here of a fort to contain cannon commanding the approaches to Falmouth Bay and Carrick Roads. The Armada of 1588 was only the beginning of attacks by the Spanish on these shores. In 1595 a party of raiders from four Spanish galleys burnt Penzance, Mousehole and Newlyn, and in 1597 only a gale prevented at attack on Falmouth, it being reported to the Privy Council that Pendennis Castle was unfit to repel troops if they landed. By February a party of 400 men had been sent under the supervision of Paul Ivey to begin work on enclosing the whole headland with a stone-revetted rampart with flanking bastions. Work was still continuing in August 1599, although the work force was then only 100 men, whilst the outer gateway seems to have only been completed in 1611. The garrison in 1599 numbered 80 musketeers, 60 pikemen, and 60 men armed with the cumbersome type of handgun called a caliver which was fired from a rest.

Gunport at
Mount Edgcumbe

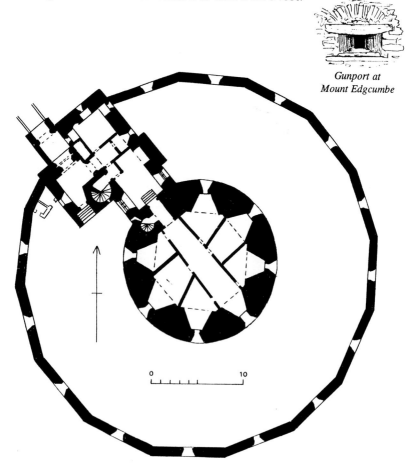

Plan of citadel of Pendennis Castle

Outer gateway at Pendennis

During the Civil War the castle was held for King Charles by the elderly John Arundel. The Duke of Hamilton was held prisoner here for 18 months, and in July 1644 Queen Henrietta Maria stayed one night before sailing to France. Prince Charles stayed for a fortnight early in 1646 before escaping to the Scilly Isles. In March that year Fairfax summoned Arundel to surrender, getting the reply that "I will here bury myself before I deliver up this castle to such as fight against his Majesty". The fortress was blockaded both by land and sea and in July Arundel sent out a message that he could not hold out much longer without relief. His 900 men were two years in arrears of pay and and were said to be living on limpets. They finally surrendered in August and marched out with the full honours of war since militarily speaking they were undefeated. Parliament was so pleased that a day of thanksgiving was held in September. The castle was maintained by Parliament and after the restoration of Charles II in 1660, Colonel William Hervey, a signatory to his father's death warrant, was incarcerated in the castle. The pamphleteer William Prynne was also held at Pendennis, and the last prisoners were French soldiers captured at the battle of Corunna in 1809. The building was damaged by lightning in 1717 and not repaired until the the 1740s. The office of Governor of Pendennis was often held by the Killigrew family, the first being John, appointed in 1546. It was Sir Peter Killigrew who founded modern Falmouth, a charter being granted by Charles II in 1661. The castle remained in military use until it became an ancient monument in state care in 1920, although it was reclaimed by the army during the 1939-45 war.

On the rocks SE of the castle lies a ruined blockhouse popularly known as Little Dennis. It is a D-shaped structure measuring 10m by 9m over walls up to 2.8m thick carrying a parapet and wall-walk about three gunports towards the sea. The entrance doorway has a pointed head and draw-bar slot and is situated in a slight re-entrant angle. The blockhouse is said to have been dismantled in 1654 but evidently saw further use as in the 18th or 19th century one large new embrasure replaced two of the originals, although their outer openings still survive.

Pendennis Castle

The fort built by Henry VIII on top of the headland comprises a round tower 17m in diameter over walls 3m thick and 10.6m high lying in the middle of a court with a low chemise wall. A stone bridge of the 1860s replaces the original drawbridge leading to a two storey square gatehouse with a four-centered arch still with the original portcullis. The Royal Arms appear on a square panel over the entrance. A rectangular wing extends from the round tower to alongside this gatehouse and projects slightly beyond the chemise wall. In the angle between the gatehouse and the wing is a staircase turret. The entrance leads through to the octagonal middle storey of the tower. Stairs lead down to a kitchen below, and there was a fighting deck above with lodgings in the wing. There was originally a powder magazine mounted on the lead roof. The chemise was once stone flagged but now has a grass surface. It is a slightly later addition and made the guns on the lowest storey of the tower redundant. The wall is no more than a massive parapet on the inside but is considerably rather higher outside.

Little Dennis Blockhouse

Little Dennis Blockhouse

Henry VIII's fort lies towards the SE end of the much larger fort of 1598-9 enclosing more than 3 acres. It is 120m wide and nearly twice as long. The SE end is pointed and there are bastions of a variety of shapes and sizes at each end and in the middle of the long sides. The entrance lies immediately north of the bastion in the middle of the SW side, from which it was covered by embrasures in the massive parapet. Externally the retaining walls descend far below the parapet to a dry ditch.

PENHALLAM   SX 225974

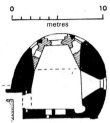

0   10
metres

A low-lying moated platform 50m by 45m bears the lower parts of the walls of the manor house of Andrew Cardinham, who died without a close heir in the mid 13th century. As revealed by excavation the layout is remarkably complete with four ranges set around a small court reached through a gatehouse on the south side. The room east of the gateway was probably a chapel. The north range contained a hall with a central hearth. The solar lay in the east range and the service rooms and kitchen lay in the double width west range.

Little Dennis Blockhouse: plan

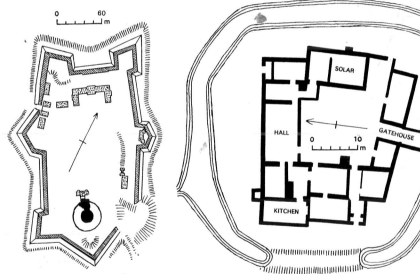

Plan of Pendennis Castle

Penhallam: Plan of moated manor house

Penhallam: manor house remains

Pengersick Castle

Pengersick Castle

PENGERSICK   SW 582284

Pengersick passed by marriage to John Beville in 1426 and then in 1476 went to the Worths. John Milliton, d1515, married the heiress Elizabeth Worth and their son John became captain of St Michael's Mount in 1522. John's son William is assumed to have added c1550-65 the embattled tower to the medieval manor house since the tower top window label bears the initial W. The house later passed to married heiresses living elsewhere and was little used. By 1794 the tower served only as a granary and hayloft. The house consisted of an inner court with external dimensions of 23m by 26m with ranges 6 or 7m wide on all four sides. The gateway faced west and the hall was in the east range with the screens passage towards its southern end. Of this there remain a block at the NW corner, the outer north wall and parts of the hall block. To the east was a larger outer court still containing the lower parts of a chapel with a priest's room west of it set towards the east end of the north side, an east range of stables with a gateway towards the south end, and another building projecting from the east half of the south side. It is uncertain how much of this existed before the tower was added to the outer court west side, forming a continuation of the hall block projecting beyond the south range of the inner court.

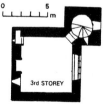

0   5
|_|_|_|_|_|m

1st STOREY   2nd STOREY   3rd STOREY   4th STOREY

Plans of Pengersick Castle

The tower is an interesting building and it is unfortunate its date of construction cannot be determined more accurately. The tower is embattled and ashlar faced and measures 7.8m square over walls 1.5m thick at basement level. There the north wall has an opening through to the adjoining range and the other three sides each have two dumbbell-shaped gunports with chamfered outer edges. The basement is reached from outside by an entrance at the foot of a spiral stair in a turret 4m square which rises above the level of the main building. A loop from the stair flanks the entrance which has a draw-bar slot and is set back in a recess, allowing a machicolation slot in the sill of a window above to command the doorway. The three upper storeys each have a large and unprotected window of four lights in the east wall and a fireplace place in a different wall at each level. The second and third storeys have latrines in the SW and NW corners respectively. The walls are thinned at each level and at the top level are not thick enough to contain a latrine, although a recess probably for a close stool is provided by the staircase rising from here to the roof.

POLRUAN   SX 123511   F

A rectangular tower stands by the shore near the mouth of the Fowey estuary and opposite St Catherine's Castle at Fowey. Although sometimes described as having been built by Henry VIII in the 1540s, its features suggest a late 15th century date. It measures 10.6m by 9m over walls mostly 1.7m thick in the lower level, whilst on the upper level all the walls except that to the NE are 1.3m thick. That side contains a fireplace and a deep embrasure with a two-light window on each storey. The entrance, with a four centred head, faces SE and there are three loops above it. The other sides have two openings each on the upper level but just one below. The staircase lies in the east corner, whilst the west corner contains a few steps down to a narrow postern. The loop above it is an oillet with a sighting slit above.

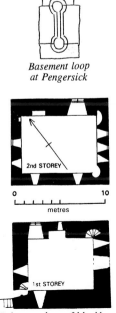

*Basement loop
at Pengersick*

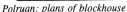

Polruan: plans of blockhouse   *Polruan Blockhouse*

RESTORMEL   SX 104614   E

At the time of the Domesday Book of 1086 the manor of Bodardle, in which Restomel lay, was held by Turstin, Sheriff of Cornwall. His son Baldwin Fitz-Turstin probably built the castle c1100 to guard a bridge that he had erected over the River Fowey. On the death of Walter Hai in 1186, the manor passed to his sister Agnes, married to Robert Fitz William, Lord of Cardinham. By 1193 their grandson Robert de Cardinan had inherited both Bodardle and Cardinham. His son Andrew left a daughter Isolda who married Thomas de Tracy and the first specific mention of the castle is when it was surrendered by de Tracy to the government led by Simon de Montfort. Isolda de Cardinan granted the castle c1270 to her overlord Richard, Earl of Cornwall and King of the Romans. His son Edmund is assumed to have built the shell wall and internal buildings between his succession to the earldom in 1272 and his death in 1299, upon which his estates reverted to the Crown. In 1337 Edward III created his eldest son Edward the Black Prince as Duke of Cornwall and ever since it has been held by the eldest son of the monarch. The Black Prince stayed in the castle in 1354 and 1365. It was later decayed and was ruinous by the 16th century. The keep was garrisoned by part of Lord Essex's Parliamentary army in 1644 but was captured in August by Sir Richard Grenville. In 1925 the Duchy of Cornwall made the Commisoners of Works guardians of the ruins. It is now administered by English Heritage.

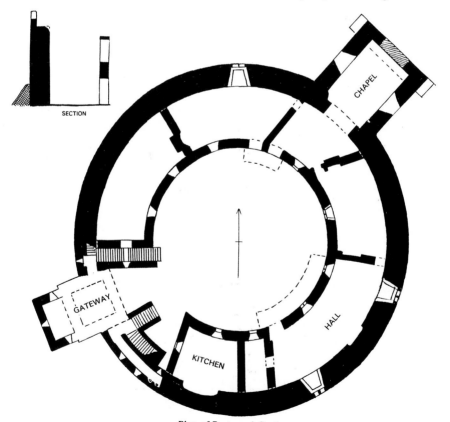

Plan of Restormel Castle

Restormel Castle

As first built c1100 the castle consisted of a ringwork with a palisade and a stone gatehouse, and a quadrangular bailey to the west. A ditch 15m wide and 4m deep surrounds the keep but little remains of any rampart or ditch around the bailey. There is no certain evidence that the bailey was ever walled in stone. A survey of 1337 mentions a hall, chapel, several chambers and a kitchen and offices in the bailey. These were probably of stone, some foundations having been traced in the area in front of the entrance to the keep, but it is possible the superstructures were of wood.

The keep is often described as a shell keep but it is an unusual one, firstly because the internal diameter of 33m makes it bigger than most other keeps of this type, and secondly because the shell wall actually rises up from the virgin ground level although from outside it appears to stand on the rampart of the ringwork. In fact most of the rampart was removed when the wall was built. The wall is 2.4m thick and has a wall-walk 8.2m above the internal courtyard level but only 6m above the top of the rampart outside. A well preserved parapet rises another 1.6m. The wall makes a straight joint against the earlier gatehouse, a now very ruinous rectangular tower with two upper rooms over a passage closed by two pairs of doors. The barbican erected in front of this tower later on is much better preserved.

Restormel Castle

Restormel Castle

The domestic buildings inside the shell are not bonded with it but are evidently of about the same date. A circular inner wall 1m thick was built 5.6m away from the shell all round, except for space left for stairs to the wall-walk on either side of the gateway, and for a pit beside the southern stairway. Cross-walls between the inner and outer walls divided up a series of arc-shaped rooms. The lower rooms have windows and doorways facing the court. The upper storey rooms have fireplaces and large windows in the shell wall, their outer openings being not far above the top of the rampart outside. The 19m long hall on the south side has a window on either side of a central fireplace. West of the hall was a lobby containing a timber stair up to it and beyond that a kitchen extending through both storeys and having a big fireplace in the outer wall. The eastern rooms were the lord's apartments set over offices. His solar lay next to the hall and had two windows facing the court, a window in the outer wall, with a stair to the wall-walk in its embrasure, and a fireplace in the northern cross-wall. The inner wall here is built over an earlier pit in the courtyard which contains a well-shaft. On the NE side of the shell-wall is a wing 9.3m wide containing a chapel on the upper storey. The embrasures remain of former two light windows on the north and south, and also a piscina, but the east window was blocked up during the Civil War when this wing was adapted to carry cannon commanding the river. A doorway on the south side of the chapel led to a long narrow timber lodging for the priest built against the outside of the shell wall. A wide arch through the shell-wall leads to the chapel from an ante-chapel or lobby which contained wooden stairs up from the court. The northern rooms were bedchambers, one for the lord next to the ante-chapel, and the other for a guest. Below the latter is a guard or barrack room with a latrine in the shell-wall. There is only one other latrine in the castle so some of the rooms must have had close stools.

ST COLUMB MAJOR   SW 912637

The 19th century rectory north of the church stands within a 40m square moated platform probably built by Ralph de Arundell, rector from 1303 to 1329. His house here, perhaps a tower like Gidleigh, withstood an attack by a mob of tinners in 1309.

ST MAWES   SW 841327   E

This castle was built on the orders of Henry VIII in 1540. By 1544 it was complete and Michael Vyvyan was appointed governor. In 1561 he was succeeded by his son Hannibal, who in turn was succeeded by Sir Francis Vyvyan in 1603. In 1632 he was tried and cashiered by the Star Chamber for "practising a variety of deceptions". When Fairfax brought up his army in March 1646 the then governor decided that the castle had been designed to protect the harbour and was not defensible against heavy cannonfire from the nearby higher ground. Accordingly he surrendered without a fight. The later governors Sir Joseph Tredinham and Sir George Nugent had seats in Parliament, the "rotten borough" of St Mawes only being abolished by the Reform Act of 1832. The office of governor itself was abolished in 1849, but a garrison remained until the castle became an ancient monument in state care in 1920, although it was again pressed into service by the military in 1939-46.

In 1599 the castle had a garrison of 100 men. In 1636 the governor was paid 3s a day, the lieutenant got 1s 6d, two gunners got 1 shilling each, and there were twelve other men paid 8d each. The intention was that local men with pikes and muskets would be pressed in to help out during times of strife. In 1609 the castle artillery comprised two sakers and an iron minion on the roof of the round tower, a culverin and six demi-culverins of iron and one of brass on the bastions plus two culverins and a brass saker among the outworks. When the castle surrendered in 1646 it was found to contain 13 pieces of ordnance and 160 small-arms.

St Mawes Castle

St Mawes Castle

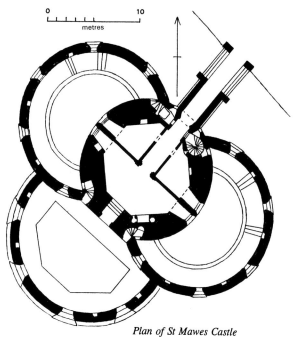

Plan of St Mawes Castle

St Mawes Castle

Blockhouse by the shore at St Mawes

The castle consists of a central round tower or keep 14.5m in diameter over walls 2.8m thick, on either side of which, facing SE and SW are bastions 17m in diameter, each with five gunports for heavy cannon. Facing SW is a third bastion also with five gunports but with its parapet at a slightly lower level. The castle is entered through a hexagonal guardhouse and then by a planked bridge over the dry moat on the NE side leading to a doorway with a four-centred arch in the keep. The approach is commanded by cross-loops with oillets on all four arms. The two slits with oillets over the entrance were for the chains of a drawbridge. Above are the Royal Arms and then on the string-course girdling the keep below the parapet is an inscription, one of several composed by the king's chaplain and antiquary John Leland upon the castle walls. This one reads "Semper Honos Henrice Tuus Laudesque Manebunt (Henry, thy honour and praises will remain for ever)".

A stair east of the entrance serves all four storeys of octagonal rooms in the keep and ends at roof level in a turret, originally with a parapet but rebuilt in the 17th century with a cupola. The lowest level of the keep was the kitchen and above that was the garrison mess room. This level was partitioned c1880 to form married quarters. From this room there is access to the courtyards of the bastions, forming the lowest gun-battery. A doorway opposite the entrance on the third storey leads out onto the SW bastion and from there curved flights of steps within the keep·walls allow access to the wall-walks on the bastions. On the SW side of the keep are four carved shields,· two of them framed in the Garter. From the gardens among the various outworks, including a hal-round bastion on the shore can be seen three unfinished Royal Arms and three more inscriptions set on the bastions. On NW bastion is "Edwardus Fama Referat Factisque Parentem (May Edward resemble his father in fame and deeds)", the SW bastion has "Honora Henricum Octavum Anglie Francie Et Hibernie Regum (Honour Henry the Eighth, most excellent King of England, France and Ireland)", and on the SE bastion is "Gaudeat Edwardo Nunc Duce Cornubia Felix "Let Cornwall rejoice that Edward is now her Duke".

ST MICHAEL'S MOUNT   SW 514299   O

A Celtic monastery is said to have occupied this tidal island from the 8th century until the 11tth century. An early cross is the only relic of that period. In the 1040s Edward the Confessor gave the mount to the abbey of Mont St Michel on a similar tidal island off the Normandy coast. Domesday Book records a priest named Brismar being in possession. A rock chamber below the floor of the choir of the present church discovered in 1720 but no longer visible may be a relic of about that time. Some time between 1135 and c1150 Bernard le Bec, Abbot of Mont St Michel erected a monastery on the summit of the rock for a prior and twelve Benedictine monks. In 1193, whilst Richard I was a prisoner in Germany, St Michael's Mount was seized and fortified by Henry de Pomeroy in support of Prince John. De Pomeroy only submitted after Richard returned to England and a strong force under Hubert Walter, Archbishop of Canterbury, was sent to take the mount.

In September 1275 an earthquake destroyed the church so that it needed rebuilding. As an alien priory subject to a mother house in France, the monastery was regarded with suspicion by Edward III and his successors after their wars against the French began in 1337. In that year an inventory of the goods and chattels of the priory was made. The priory was not wealthy and they were not worth much, and by 1362, as a result of plague, there were only a prior and two monks left in the monastery. When Henry V began his campaign which led to the victory of Agincourt in 1415 the priory was suppressed and its lands granted to the Brigittine Abbey of Syon at Twickenham which he had recently founded. Henry VI confirmed this grant in 1424. In 1425 the Bishop of Exeter decided that three chaplains should live in the priory in place of the three monks formerly living there. In 1473 St Michael's Mount was captured by the Earl of Oxford in support of the deposed Henry VI against Edward IV. The earl and his men disguised themselves as pilgrims and overcame the small garrison and clergy. The earl had family connections in Cornwall and was able to stock the fortress with provisions and munitions. Eventually the earl was obliged to surrender after many of his force of about 80 were induced to desert by promises of bribes and favours. He later escaped from Hamme Castle near Calais and in 1485 helped Henry Tudor defeat Richard III and and take his throne.

St Michael's Mount

Church at St Michael's Mount

In 1497 the Yorkist pretender Perkin Warbeck landed in Cornwall and was admitted to St Michael's Mount by the priests. Warbeck left his wife Lady Catherine Gordon, a noted beauty and a relative of James IV of Scots, in the Mount. She was captured there and sent to King Henry at Taunton after her husband's rebellion petered out and he surrendered. They remained at court but Perkin was executed in 1499 after involvement in another conspiracy. The priory was dissolved by Henry VIII in 1535 and Humphrey Arundell was appointed Captain of the Mount. He was a Catholic and became one of the leaders of the rebellion against the new prayer book in 1549. At the time he was absent and it was neccsary for him to besiege the place and take it from a party of local gentlemen who had taken refuge there. Arundell was hanged at Tyburn after capture at Launceston.

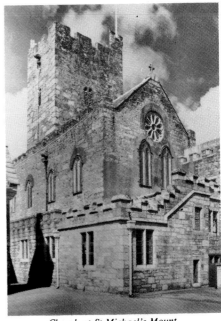

Church at St Michael's Mount

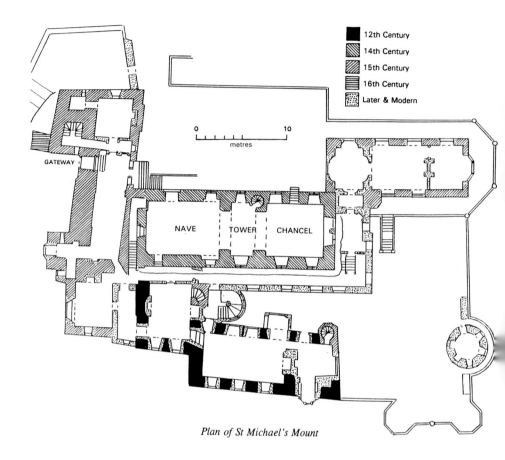

12th Century
14th Century
15th Century
16th Century
Later & Modern

0   10
metres

GATEWAY

NAVE   TOWER   CHANCEL

Plan of St Michael's Mount

St Michael's Mount was subsequently held by a succession of local gentry who were required to maintain there a garrison of five men and a priest. Elizabeth I eventually granted the stronghold to Robert Cecil, her Secretary of State. A lease was granted by him to Sir Arthur Harris from 1596 until his death in 1628. He often petioned the Privy Council for more guns and supplies for the defence of St Michael's Mount. Passing ships were required to strike their topsails in acknowledgement that they were subject to the Governor of the castle. In 1640 the 2nd Earl of Salibury sold the castle to Sir Francis Basset. When the Civil War broke out in 1642 he strengthened the defences and installed a garrison of twelve men and a gunner. In 1644 the garrison was increased to fifty men on the orders of King Charles, Francis being knighted the same year for his services as Sheriff and Commander-in-Chief of royal forces in Cornwall. In 1646 the future Charles II stayed at the Mount on his way to seeking safety in the Scilly Isles. Sir Arthur Basset surrendered St Michael's Mount in April that year to Parliamentary forces after some of his garrison began to desert and others were captured unarmed in the streets of Marazion. Sir Arthur and his officers were allowed to go to the Scilly Isles.

In 1647 Colonel John St Aubyn was appointed as Captain of the Mount and in 1649 he helped put down an insurrection in Cornwall. In 1659 St Aubyn purchased the Mount from the now-impoverished Bassets. His arms together with those of his wife (a Godolphin) appear over the entrance. He died in 1684, supposedly drowned whilst crossing the causeway on horseback. His son was created a baronet by Charles II, the first of five Sir John Aubyns to own the Mount. However they preferred to live at their house of Clowance at Crowan near Camborne until it was destroyed by fire in the early 19th century and they transferred to the Mount. This family still live there, but since 1954 as tenants of the National Trust. Queen Victoria and Prince Albert paid a visit in 1846 whilst cruising on the royal yacht although at the time none of the family were in residence as the will of the fifth baronet was still in dispute. During the Second World war the island was manned by a platoon of infantry and three blockhouses, now removed, were built at the base of the island.

The 14th century church stands in the middle of the summit of the rocky tidal island and measures 19m long by 5.6m wide internally. A narrow central tower divides the nave from the choir. On the tower is a beacon with a transom and a basin-shaped floor known as St Michael's Chair. At one time pilgrims coming to the island insisted on climbing onto this perilous perch as part of their devotions. The church has late medieval windows of two lights and is entered by a doorway in the nave north wall, now facing a terrace 10m wide. A detached late 15th century Lady Chapel NE of the church was remodelled in the 18th century and now contains the Blue Drawing Room. A narrow terrace surrounds this part. Just 6m to the south of the church, some of which is taken up by a 19th century corridor against the church south wall, lies the refectory block. The walling here may be 12th century but the features are 19th century, with the Chevy Chase Room above the Garrison Room. East of this is another 19th century terrace with rooms underneath. West of the church is a range of apartments probably of 15th century date since the entrance arch looks like work of that period. The north end projects forward and there is another projection further south so some sort of covering fire in front of the entrance was posssible. There are further rooms between the south end of this block and the former refectory, the monastic kitchen probably being located here.

St Michael's Mount: west front

Interior of church at
St Michael's Mount

Tintagel Castle: Inner Ward

TINTAGEL   SX 050890   E

In 1227 Henry III created his brother Richard Earl of Cornwall, Richard having had the lands three years earlier. In 1236 the earl exchanged lands with Gervase de Tintagel and thus obtained possession of the castle site. It is uncertain whether the site had ever been fortified up to then, although as the tenants of the manor of Bossiney which included Tintagel styled themselves "of Tintagel" they may have lived there. The Celtic missionary St Juliot founded a church and monastery on the headland at Tintagel c500AD, but by 1086 the monastery had gone leaving probably only a small chapel as a reminder of its existance. Despite all the Authurian legends concerning Tintagel and the suitability of the summit of the headland as the site of a stronghold, there is no evidence of a fortress then existing here. It is possible, however, that Reginald, Earl of Cornwall from 1140 to 1175 fortified the site. Earl Richard is assumed to have erected the surrounding walls of all three courts of the castle but it is unlikely that he lived there much. He may have been stimulated to fortify the site in honour of the Arthurian legends then popular since the castle can never have had a strategic importance. In 1257 Earl Richard was elected King of the Romans and attempted to rule much of what is now Germany. After his son Edmund died heirless in 1299 his estates reverted to the Crown. Edward II made his favourite Piers Gaveston Earl of Cornwall, and the earldom was later held by John of Eltham, brother of Edward III. Neither of these lived in Cornwall and the latter had the great hall at Tintagel unroofed, presumably so the timbers could be used elsewhere.

In 1337 Edward III created his eldest son Edward, later in adulthood known as the Black Prince, Duke of Cornwall. A survey then conducted shows the castle as ruinous but by 1345 a smaller new hall had been built on the site of the old one with a pantry, buttery and kitchen. However, the castle saw little or no use as a lordly residence. It was used as a prison for political prisoners at the end of the 14th century and some alterations seem to be of about that period, but the castle then rapidly decayed. In c1540 John Leland described the castle as ruinous and deserted.

The castle protected the approach to an almost isolated headland with a summit about 200m across in each direction. On the summit and on the eastern slopes are various huts and small crudely built chambers which are relics of the early monastery, a chapel with a west porch being recognisable on the east side of the summit. The summit can only be reached by going through the inner ward, an enclosure perched on a shelf below the SE corner. This inner ward is now a triangle with the longest side extending for 60m but it cannot be said what its original shape was or what defences it possessed towards the approach. This part of the ward and the causeway that linked it to the two wards on the landward side collapsed into the sea during the later part of the medieval period. It is thus necessary for modern visitors to descend to a wooden bridge above the rocky shore-level isthmus which is now all that connects the headland (known as "The Island") to the mainland.

The inner ward has a curtain wall about 1.1m thick meandering irregularly along its northern side. Where the path to the summit of the island pierces the wall with a arch the wall head survives complete and has a parapet rising up in steps without a wall-walk. This wall is probably mid 13th century but the projecting latrine east of the ach and the buildings it served are probably of c1400. The NE side of the court was formed by a hall block 11m wide and over 26m long, possibly of pre-13th century date. Only the NE wall facing the sea and shored up with later buttresses stands much above the footings. In the mid 14th century a narrower new hall was built on this site and about half a century later it was subdivided. At that time another block containing two rooms was built in the middle of the present courtyard space.

Tintagel Castle: the upper and lower wards

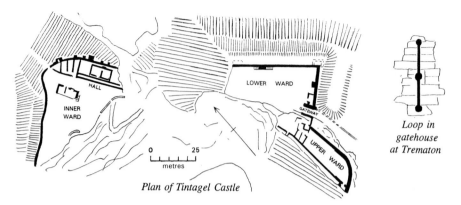

Plan of Tintagel Castle

Loop in gatehouse at Trematon

The lower ward measures about 50m by 20m. The NW and SW sides face cliffs to the sea. The NE and SE sides have straight curtain walls about 1.2m and 1.5m thick respectively probably of mid 13th century date. The slight remains of two rectangular turrets at either end of the NE side are probably mid 14th century. This side also has stairs up to the wall-walk and is protected by a ditch with an outer bank. A much wider ditch protects the SE side, just a causeway being left as the approach to a gateway at the south corner. Beside the gateway steps lead up to the upper ward, which commands the approach to the gateway from a rocky ridge west of it. This ward has a curtain wall up to 2m thick curving round its east and south sides. The ward is 50m long but now nowhere wider than 10m, being closed off on the west by a thin wall with latrines at each end. This wall is assumed to have been built in the 14th century after a collapse of the cliff had destroyed much of this ward. Chambers across the ward near its northern end are thought to be of c1400.

TREGONY   SW 926449

Nothing now remains visible of a castle built c1193 by Henry de Pomeroy in support of Prince John, ruler of Cornwall during Richard I's absence on crusade. It is thought to have been rebuilt in the 14th century and still existed in 1540. There is a further mention of the castle and its well in 1640.

Tintagel Castle

TREMATON   SX 410579

Earl Robert de Mortain built this castle, mentioned in Domesday Book in 1087. It is said that the stone walls date from the time of Reginald de Valletort, who held the castle during Richard I's reign, but the crossloop on the keep parapet and the gatehouse were probably added by Roger de Valletort, upon whose death in 1270 Trematon reverted to Richard, Earl of Cornwall. The castle was granted by Edward II to his favourite Piers Gaveston in 1307. In 1315 Peter Corbet and Henry de Pomeroy claimed possesion as descendants of two Valletort heiresses but they were unsuccessful. Edward III granted Trematon to his brother John of Eltham. After he died in 1335 it was granted to Edward the Black Prince, and it then became part of the Duchy of Cornwall created for him in 1337. The prince may never have visited the castle but he had it surveyed that year. This report mentions a hall, a kitchen and a block containing two storeys of lodgings, all these being of timber with plaster infilling and said to be the work of Earl Edmund, who held the castle from 1272 to 1299. A chapel within the gatehouse is also referred to. The buildings were in good condition and an annual sum of £3 was considered enough for maintenance.

When a French raid on the coast was expected in 1385 the sum of £20 was spent on repairing the defences. Richard II granted Trematon to John Holland, Earl of Huntingdon, executed in 1400 by Henry IV. In 1425 Henry V granted it to the earl's widow Elizabeth and her second husband Sir John Cornewall. It reverted to the Crown on Sir John's death in 1443. Edward IV carried out a few repairs and the castle was in use as a prison during Leland's visit in 1540. Sir Richard Grenville took refuge in the castle during the Arundell rebellion of 1549. Sir Richard was seized when he slipped out of a postern gateway to negotiate with the rebels. He and his wife were stripped of their possessions, even the clothes they were wearing, the castle was captured, and Sir Richard was taken off to Launceston. Elizabeth I granted a 21 year lease of the castle to Thomas Brishowe, after which it was granted to the Carews. By that time the internal buildings were ruined although the castle continued to accommodate prisoners and was used to store treasure brought back by Sir Francis Drake from the Indes. The castle was briefly occupied during the 1640s but saw no action. A Parliamentary report shows it still held prisoners in 1650.

Shell Keep at Trematon Castle

Trematon: looking down into the bailey

The castle consists of a well-preserved shell keep on a mound high above the Lynher river with a bailey extending to the SW. The shell wall is 2.4m thick above a substantial battered plinth and 6.8m high to a wall-walk which still retains its parapet with merlons 1.7m high, one cross-loop with a triangular foot being preserved on the west side. The oval court inside measures 22.6m by 17.6m and has slight traces of former lean-to buildings. There are no latrines or staircases, the only opening in the shell-wall being a round arched doorway 2.2m wide with a drawbar slot. The bailey extends for 90m from the keep and is 70m wide. On the east side the curtain still extends up the motte slope to the keep. There is a postern on the NW at the foot of the mound, but there are no towers or turrets apart from the gatehouse at the foot of the mound on the east side. The gatehouse is a fine structure about 10m square projecting entirely outside the curtain. The approach is commanded by two arrow-loops and the passage, which rises steeply, was closed by portcullises at the inner and outer ends and a two-leaved door in the middle, the inner section being flanked by tiny guardrooms in the wall thickness. A spiral stair leads up from the court to two upper rooms both with fireplaces with stiff-leaf capitals. The lower room has mural chambers on each side and the upper room has a passage leading to a latrine. The curtain wall curving round from the gatehouse along the south side of the bailey to a sharp turn at the SW corner was demolished to give a view of the sea from a house built in 1808 as a residence for Benjamin Tucker, Surveyor-General of the Duchy of Cornwall, who held the castle on a 99 year lease. The remaining parts of the bailey walls still have original parapets with narrow crenels. See pages 6,7 and 9.

TRURO   SW 823451

Nothing remains of a castle said to have been built by Richard de Lucy during King Stephen's reign upon Castle Hill but footings of a shell keep with a forebuilding were revealed in 1840, after which the site was a cattlemarket. William of Worcester described the castle as ruinous in 1478.

UPTON   SX 245785

This site lies above the north bank of the River Lynher on the NE slopes of Bodmin Moor. There are remains of a drystone hall 13m by 8m internally plus another building, together taking up much of the space within a court 25m by 23m with a thick outer drystone wall with one projection perhaps making the site of a latrine. This was presumably the seat of the de Upton family in the 12th century.

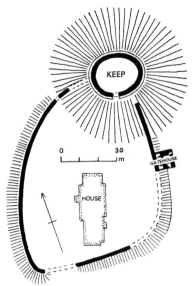

Plan of Trematon Castle

VERYAN   SW 909388

High above the east side of a stream running to the short 0.5km to the south at Carne Beath is a ringwork. The site slopes considerably uphill to the east, where a rampart closes off the site from higher ground beyond.

WEEK ST MARY   236978

West of the church are worn-down remains of a ringwork about 22m across possibly dating back to the time of Richard Fitz-Turold, Steward to Robert de Mortain in the late 11th century. There are traces of a rectangular bailey to the east. In the 12th century the manor was held by the de Wyke family as tenants of the Cardinhams, passing in the mid 13th century to the Blanchminsters, and later to the Coleshills.

Town gateway, Launceston

OTHER MEDIEVAL FORTIFIED SITES IN CORNWALL

CARMINOW   Part of a moated medieval house survived until the 19th century.
EASTLEIGH BERRYS SS 244067. Ditches define a slighted or unfinished motte now only 2m high with an oval bailey to the NE and another bailey beyond.
LANHERNE   SW 873674 A broad ditch remains on the west side of the house, which was the seat of the Arundell family, but has been a convent since 1794.
LEE SS 228122 This house near Morwenstow has traces of a possible former moat.
SHEVIOCK   In 1336 Edward licensed John Dawney to crenellate his manor house.
ST IVES   Leland mentions a blockhouse at St Ives which has vanished.
TRUTHWALL SW 528324 In 1335 Edward III licensed Ralph de Bloyou to crenellate his manor house here. There are no remains of that period.
There are said to have once been towers at the manor houses of Boconnoc, near Lostwithiel, Park, near Egloshayle, and Trerice at Newlyn East.

GAZETTEER OF CASTLES IN DEVON

BAMPTON   SS 959225   F

On top of a steep hill above the River Batham is a mound rising 9m to a dished summit about 30m by 25m. The mound stands in the west corner of a quadrangular bailey platform 90m long by 65m wide. There is a formidable ditch and counterscarp on the NE side but the defences are hardly visible on the vulnerable NW side. It was probably this site which Robert de Bampton fortified against King Stephen in 1136. The garrison, led by Robert's son, surrendered after a messenger sent out of the castle to summon help was caught and hanged within view of the ramparts. Robert was a younger son of Walter of Douai, holder of this estate at the time of Domesday and who died c1100, by which time the castle is assumed to have been built. The Cogans held the barony from 1267 and Richard Cogan was licensed by Edward III to embattle his house at Bampton in 1336. The slight traces of a building perhaps about 17m long by 8m wide on the motte summit may be a relic of it. See page 5.

BARNSTAPLE   SS 556334   F

In 1087 Domesday Book refers to the destruction of 23 houses to make room for a castle beside the River Taw. It was then held by Judhael, who lived until 1113. The Gesta Stephani (life of King Stephen) describes the castle as weak and powerless but it was later strengthened by the erection of a stone keep, perhaps by Henry de Tracy, who was succeeded by his son Oliver in 1165. Descriptions of two gates destroyed in 1842 and 1852 suggest they were Norman, although they may have formed part of the town defences. Excavations in 1927 revealed that the tree-clad motte 8m high had a clay-set revetment and on the summit were found footings of what were interpreted as a shell wall 2.7m thick enlosing a court 14m across with an outer mantlet wall 1m thick set 1m away from the main wall. The bailey lay to the SW, and there may have been an outer bailey as well. In 1228 the Sheriff of Devon was ordered to supervise the the reduction of the height of the castle walls to 3m, evidently a reaction to unauthorised building work. An inquision on the death of Henry de Tracy in 1274 refers to a hall, chamber, kitchen and other buildings on the motte. In 1333 there is a mention of providing a chaplain for a chapel noted in 1281.

The motte summit at Barnstaple

*The mid 16th century hall
block at Berry Pomeroy*

The gatehouse at Berry Pomeroy

BERRY POMEROY   SX 840623   E

The Pomeroy family had a residence on the site of the present manor house in the village from the time of Ralph de la Pomerai, rated in Domesday Book as the fifth largest landowner in Devon. In 1207 John Pomeroy paid King John 10 marks for a licence to enclose a park. His son Henry was Sheriff of Devon and Governor of Exeter Castle in the 1230s. A "hall with chambers" is mentioned in a survey of 1293. Richard Pomeroy was knighted at the coronation of Elizabeth of York, queen of Henry VII, and served twice as Sheriff of Devon. He probably erected the present castle on a promontory above the Gatcombe Brook and excavations have not found any certain evidence of anything older on the site. In 1496 his widow Elizabeth was given an extensive dower including "a great chamber beyond the castle gate with the cellar on the left of the gate, with two chambers beyond and belonging to the said chamber, a kitchen, larderhouse and a chamber beyond the kitchen". In 1548 Richard's grandson Thomas sold the castle and its lands to Protector Somerset for £4,000. Thomas Pomeroy was imprisoned in the Tower of London after taking part in the west country rebellion of 1549 against the new English prayer book but escaped his sentence of hanging, drawing and quartering.

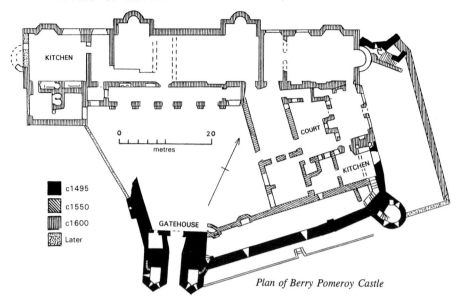

Plan of Berry Pomeroy Castle

Sir Edward Somerset, son of the Lord Protector, lived at the castle from c1554 until his death in 1593. He built a new kitchen wing behind the older ramparts and a fine hall block at right angles to it. His son, another Edward, was created a baronet by James I in 1611. This Edward erected a long new range across the whole north side of the site but the full scheme including a new west range and terraces overlooking the stream was never completed and the west part of the north range was later only used by servants. The family had over-reached themselves and in the 1690s Sir Edward Seymour, Speaker of the House of Commons, Commissioner of the Treasury and Comptroller of the Household, transferred to a more modest house at Maiden Bradley in Wiltshire which was more convient for travelling to London. A steward is said to have occupied part of the ruined castle until the 1790s. In the 1970s the eighteenth Duke of Somerset placed the ruins in the care of the State.

Machicolation over the gateway at Berry Pomeroy

Facing the south approach is a curtain wall about 40m long with the U-shaped St Margaret's tower at the east end and the gatehouse at the west end. The features of the tower and gatehouse suggest a date of c1485-95 and the curtain seems to be contemporary, as does the short fragment of curtain walling which adjoins the NW corner of the gatehouse and contains a latrine serving its upper storey. The curtain is about 1.5m thick and is backed by a rampart reached by stairs beside the gate. The gatehouse passage is flanked by guard rooms within prow-fronted towers. These rooms are only reached from above and have towards the field unusual loops with an oillet half way up a vertical slit. A flat four-centred arch thrown between the towers high up has a machicolation behind it. St Margaret's Tower is 5.3m wide and boldly projects 5.2m towards the former dry moat. It too has a basement only reached from above and fitted with slits with double oillets for hand-guns set above square double splayed loops for small cannon. No medieval domestic buildings remain. On the north side of the court is a very ruined range of c1600-10 nearly 80m long by 13m wide. The hall lay in the middle and had three windows overlooking the drop to the stream. On this side the range has four projecting bays, the middle bays being in the form of half-rounds projecting from rectangles. Towards the court was a loggia or passage with five arches. The west end projects well beyond the line of the original west curtain wall and contained a kitchen and bakery. Tusks on the standing parts indicate a wide range was intended to have continued south from here to form a west range perched dramatically upon the slope. The east of the north range end contained a parlour. This part formed the north wing of a set of four ranges of apartments set around a small inner court. This part is better preserved, particularly the original hall block of c1560 forming the west range of this court. South of this earlier hall were the buttery and pantry and then the south range adjoining it, set behind the older rampart, contained other service rooms including a kitchen in the SE corner with a fireplace with two ovens. These parts have large mullion-and-transom windows of four lights and high chimney stacks. The east range of this court is later.

Berry Pomeroy Castle

Bickleigh Castle

BICKLEIGH   SS 937068

Bickleigh was a secondary seat of the Courtenays, Earls of Devon. It was a fortified house with a moat, now mostly filled in, and a rectangular gatehouse of the late 14th or early 15th century on the east side. On the east face of the gatehouse are the arms of Sir William Carew's younger brother Thomas, who eloped with and married the heiress Elizabeth Courtenay. To escape the joint wrath of both families Thomas joined the army that defeated the Scots at Flodden in 1514 and is said to have distinguished himself in that fight. Another set of arms refers to Sir Henry Carew and his wife, one of the Mohuns. Sir Henry repaired the gatehouse after the castle was captured by Sir Thomas Fairfax and slighted by order of Parliament, the north and west ranges of the courtyard building then being destroyed. The four-light windows on the second storey are the work of Sir Henry. On the east side the passage outer arch is flanked by buttresses dying into the wallface below these windows, and there are projections at each end of this side. Beside the river nearby is an Early Norman chapel with a 15th century roof. When the estate was sold by the Carews to the Harpers in 1922 the house was a farm and the chapel was used as a cattle byre. Bickleigh later passed to the Hensons and is now owned by the Boxalls.

COLCOMBE   SY 247948

A farm near the east bank of the Umborne Brook has remains of a manor house of the Courtenays, Earls of Devon, although the Poles also once owned it. Part is incorporated in the existing house but most of it ruinous and consists of a long range with a kitchen at its north end. There are 15th century windows and mullioned windows of later date. The site is said to have been moated but there is nothing else in the way of defensive features.

Compton Castle

The NE tower at Compton

COMPTON   SX 865649   O

The de Compton family held lands here from the Bishop of Exeter during King Stephen's reign. In 1954 the National Trust rebuilt the original great hall built by Geoffrey Gilbert in the 1330s. He obtained the manor in the 1320s by marrying Joan, daughter and heiress of William de Compton, and his descendants continued to live at Compton until 1800. They recovered the estate in 1930, and later presented it to the National Trust, the rebuilding of the hall being part of an agreement which allows them to remain as tenants. The west wing is mid 15th century and the rest is all the work of John Gilbert c1500-20. He converted the then unfortified manor house into a stronghouse, not capable of withstanding a siege or bombardment since it is overlooked by higher ground immediately outside the walls, but impressive to look at and able to offer resistance to a raiding party, the French having recently raided Teignmouth. The most famous member of the family was Sir Humphrey Gilbert, half brother of Sir Walter Raleigh. Sir Humphrey was probably born at Greenway, then seat of the junior branch of the Gilberts, and was lost at sea in September 1583 whilst returning from Newfoundland, being commemorated by a tablet in the chapel.

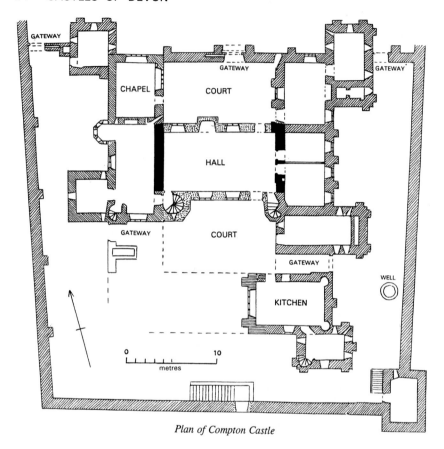

Plan of Compton Castle

The hall is 12.4m long by 6m wide and is of four bays with two-light windows. The east bay forms the screens passage with twin doors leading to the pantry and buttery which are part of an east range rebuilt in 1500-20. The west bay of the hall is the dais end and has a lobby on the south side containing a stair to the private rooms on the upper storey of the mid 15th century west range. The lower rooms here are a withdrawing room backing against the hall and having a later bay window on the west side, plus a vaulted chapel north of this, entered from the north court and having a large north end four-light window protected by a projecting grille. Originally the west range continued further south but beyond a side entrance flanked by a tower 5.2m square it no longer survives. The 16th century remodelling provided a buttressed tower or projection on the east side, with an entrance passage between it and a kitchen in the east end of a new south range, the western portion of which has gone. This south range enclosed a court 7m wide south of the hall, whilst a curtain wall with a gateway in the middle with a portcullis closed off a north court 6.2m wide, both courts being 12.4m long. At each corner a tower-like wing was added, those on the north front being about 5m wide and having buttresses set back from the corners. Each has a box machicolation high up on each outer face but there are no battlements. The NE tower and the SE tower are both rectangular rather than square like the NW tower. The SW tower no longer exists.

Compton Castle

Closely surrounding this complex, except on the north side, which remains open, is an outer wall about 1.3m thick with a flanking tower of its own at the SE corner. Stairs beside it lead to an upper room. North of this tower is a well. On the north this outer court could be entered though gateways on either side of the corner towers of the main building. The outer court was not in itself really defensible because the land outside was at a rather high level. Instead it formed a confined killing-ground covered all round by ports for handguns in the towers of the main house.

North Front of Compton Castle

DARTMOUTH   SX 887504   E

Dartmouth was a major port in the medieval period. It was the mustering place for the fleet that set out on the Second Crusade in 1147, and the 31 ships it sent towards Edward III's siege of Calais in 1346 was bettered only by Yarmouth and Fowey. From that period onwards there was a serious risk of sea-borne reprisal raids on the town which had grown up on the west bank of the estuary, especially since the Dartmouth captains had a tendency to attack Breton ships. Edward III sent commissioners to review the defences of Dartmouth and other ports. By 1388, during the period when John Hawley was mayor and after a certain amount of royal chivvying, there was under construction "a fortalice by the sea at the entrance of that part for the defence of the town and of the ships of other parts of the realm which touch there". This castle lay not in the town itself but on a headland at the mouth of the harbour over 1km to the SE. A deep ditch and two sections of walling each about 40m long facing west and a shorter wall facing south closed off a headland of irregular shape with the church of St Petrox in the northern part of it. The south wall of this courtyard castle still remains 6m high with one round SW corner tower. The turret by the gate in the middle of the west side and much of the walling there has gone, as has a NW corner tower. In 1403 a raiding party of Bretons was defeated not far away but after John Hawley died in 1408 the castle seems to have been abandoned, the townsfolk despairing of the large cost of manning and maintenance. The Carew lords of Stoke Fleming later had a residence in the enclosure. It was described as deserted by John Leland in 1539 although ruins of still stood in 1822.

In 1402 the merchant John Corp was granted a licence "to crenellate a lodging of his by the entrance of the port of the town for defence against the King's enemies". This may have been at Paradise Point on the north side of Warfleet Creek, where a strong round tower was demolished in 1855 to make way for a house called Ravensbury although this tower was probably of later date (see also page 65).

The 14th century defences at Dartmouth Castle

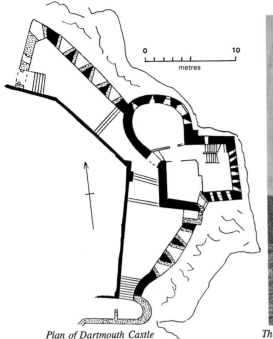

Plan of Dartmouth Castle

The 15th century round tower at Dartmouth

During the 15th century it seems a watch was kept upon Gallant's Bower on the hill above the old castle and in 1462 Edward IV granted £30 from the customs of Exeter and Dartmouth towards the expense of maintaining a chain which was stretched across the harbour mouth. By 1481 the townfolk had under construction a fort at the waters' edge to guard the chain. It is situated east of St Petrock's Church beside the older castle. Edward IV renewed the annuity of £30 from customs and added an additional £30 for five years to encourage completion of the work. In 1486 Henry VII increased the maintenance sum to £40 per annum, and this remained in force until the early 19th century. The fort or "strong tower" was originally designed as a round structure of irregular shape about 7m across over walls 1m thick. Before it was completed work was begun on an adjoining rectangular block again or irregular shape but roughly 9m by 7m. Finally short lengths of low curtain were built on either side, now pierced by later embrasures for three guns on the south side and up to five on the north. The two towers are of three storeys with gunports commanding the river mouth. The lowest level is a basement built against a rock ledge on the west. Here the cannon were mounted, the upper floors being accommodation for the garrison. The gunports are rectangular and were closed by external shutters. The entrance lies at the level above which is divided by partitions in a central passage with one room in the round tower and two rooms and a timber stair in the rectangular tower. The third storey is undivided and has a stair in the wall on the south side up to the roof. The work progressed slowly and not until 1493-4 were beams and lead purchased for flooring and roofing the rectangular tower. Meanwhile weapons were purchased and in 1491 four watchmen were paid 6s 8d a month to guard the castle. Six small boats called cobbles were hired at 48s per month each to carry the chain across the river. In 1596-7 money was spent on repairing the bridge over the ditch at the entrance and on inserting three more gunports in the rectangular tower.

Dartmouth Castle from the sea

In 1509-10 there is a record of an indenture between Henry VIII and the bailiff of Dartmouth for a tower to be built and furnished with artillery at the harbour mouth. This may be the round blockhouse called Bayard's Cove Castle at the south end of the town. It is mentioned as the "New Castle" in a lease of 1537, and in 1539 Leland described it as "a fair bulwark, built of late". An open court rather than a tower, it has a wall-walk and remains of a corbelled parapet over a series of gunports for eleven cannon. The stairs to the wall-walk climb up over the mutilated entrance. The gunports are larger than those of the castle but still early in type being designed for flat-bed guns rather than those mounted on wheeled carriages which was the norm by the end of Henry VIII's reign. There are slight traces of lean-to buildings against the rockface at the back. This fort was briefly used again in 1940 as a machine-gun post but found to have too restricted a field of fire from its gunports.

During the Civil War Dartmouth declared for Parliament but was captured by Prince Maurice in 1643 after a month's siege. The Royalists held a garrison of 500 men here and built outlying earthen forts with flanking angle bastions on Gallant's Bower above the castle and at Mount Ridley above Kingswear. These defences were stormed by a Parliamentary force led by Sir Thomas Fairfax in January 1646. The Gallant's Bower fort was then slighted but the castle was maintained against possible attacks by sea. Custody of the castle was taken over by the Crown under Charles II but the town retained the £40 per annum from the customs for castle maintenance until 1828.

Machicolations at Dartmouth Castle

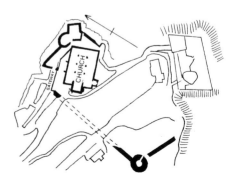

Site plan of Dartmouth Castle

Bayard's Castle, Dartmouth

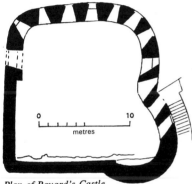

Plan of Bayard's Castle

Bayard's Castle, Dartmouth

A large granite-faced 19th century battery above the bathing beach now lies on the site of Lamberd's Bulwark, mentioned in 1545, and described in a report found on a captured Spanish spy in 1599 as able to mount six or eight pierces of artillery. This bulwark was rebuilt in stone in 1690, an additional fort to defend Dartmouth against Dutch naval raids having been ordered in 1672. The defences of all these forts soon decayed. In 1717 a survey by Colonel Lilly of fortifications in this district noted there were 58 guns at Dartmouth but only one had a serviceable carriage. Two elderly gunners looked after the mouldering stores and the last remaining 6m long length of the harbour chain. Lamberd's Bulwark was again rebuilt in 1747 and then mounted twelve guns in two tiers. There was still a garrison of three men at Dartmouth in 1886 and the castle was used by the local militia. It became an ancient monument in 1907 but was used again by the army in the Second World War. The tip of the headland enclosed by the 14th century walls has a battery of the 1860s on the site of an 18th century battery. Until recently it was used as a restaurant.

DURPLEY   SS 429125

The earthwork known as Durpley Castle near Shebbear is perched on a hill above two streams. It consists of a small ringwork 16m in diameter with a rampart rising 3.5m above the interior and 5.5m above the surrounding rock-cut ditch. The only easy approach to the site is from the west, where there is a crescent-shaped bailey 42m by 25m with a rampart rising 3m above a ditch with a strong counterscarp bank.

EXETER   SX 921929   V

Exeter was fortified by the Romans with a stone wall and it appears that this was still defensible in 1068 when the city defied King William I. The late King Harold's mother Githa had much influence here and when William tried to intimidate the defenders by parading a blinded hostage the only response was a rude gesture. After eighteen days of siege the city, then the tenth largest in England, was surrendered on generous terms under which the citizens were not to be harmed or their annual tribute increased. William honoured the terms but immediately built a castle to control the city and put it in the care of Baldwin de Brione, created Sheriff of Devon.

The castle was positioned in the north corner of the city, the highest available site, and consisted of a nearly square inner ward with earth ramparts, those on the NE and NW sides covering the old Roman walls. The 7m square gatehouse still standing on the SE side faced towards an outer ward of which little now remains. The gatehouse is assumed to have been built at the time of the foundation of the castle since the triangular-headed windows of the upper storey suggests that Saxon masons were employed upon it. This upper storey has no other features and it is unclear how it was entered. There are pilaster buttresses at the corners and semi-circular gateway arches of two orders. The arches were closed by pairs of doors. Two short walls on the outer face carry a third arch higher up forming a sort of barbican covering the inner part of a gap in the approach ramp spanned by a drawbridge. In the 13th century the gateway was blocked and a small postern doorway inserted through the side-wall to the NE. A hole in one jamb of this postern looks like a later gunport.

Exeter Castle, showing the Early Norman Gateway

Exeter Castle

It is uncertain when the curtain wall was built around the inner ward. The NE and NW sides could have had stone walls from the start, using the Roman walls buried in the banks as a foundation. The square Athelstan's Tower with mid-wall pilasters at the west corner looks early and there is herringbone masonry, another sign of early date, in the inner face of the northern curtain wall. The inner ward certainly appears to have been entirely stone walled by 1136 when Baldwin de Redvers, a supporter of the Empress Maud, held the castle against a siege by King Stephen lasting three months. A tunnel discovered in the 1930s running from outside the city wall towards the castle is thought to be a relic of an attempt by Stephen's engineers to undermine the stone walls. The ringwork known as Danescastle which lay nearby at SX 919934 until destroyed in the 19th century may have been King Stephen's siege camp. Baldwin was eventually captured after his other castle at Carisbrooke on the Isle of Wight surrendered to the King after the water supply failed. He was exiled and forfeited but was later restored to his estates and title of Earl of Devon.

From the time of Henry II onwards the castle was retained by the Crown. The Pipe Rolls record over £200 being spent on its buildings in the 1170s. Nearly £50 was spent on the king's chamber in 1180-1. In 1207-8, under King John, over £50 was spent on the ditches and on transporting stone and lime. It is probable that the outer ward was then given a curtain wall, although only a fragment of it now remains. The tower with pilaster buttresses rising from a broad circular base by the east corner of the inner ward also probably dates from this period, the pilasters recalling the much superior Lunn's Tower built by King John at Kenilworth. The tower is now reduced to a stump surmounted by a modern brick parapet. On the NE side is a second tower of this type, 5.5m in diameter above a battered plinth from which again rise thin pilasters. Two storeys remain, the lower one now having a wide modern arch plus two enlarged original loops. In 1217 John's widow Queen Isabella took refuge in the castle. In 1228 Henry III built a new postern at the north corner, now vanished, but the work was perhaps inadequately done as it was remodelled in 1238-9. Old drawings show another long vanished tower at the south corner, near the gatehouse. Near the east corner stood a chapel of St Mary, possibly original 11th century work.

Plan of Exeter Castle

Corner tower at Exeter

In later years the castle remained important as an administrative centre but the defences were allowed to decay. In 1274 it was reported that the towers were roofless and that part of the curtain had collapsed, whilst in 1309 there was a report of three towers having fallen. The castle formed part of the Duchy of Cornwall created by Edward III for his son Edward the Black Prince. Richard III visited Exeter not long after his coronation at York in 1483. He became very alarmed after being told that the castle was called Rougemont (Red Mount, from its red sandstone walls) for he took that to be the same as Richmond and had been told by an Irish Bard he would not live long after he saw Richmond, this scene being recalled by Shakespeare in the play Richard III. Richard was indeed defeated and killed in 1485 by the forces of Henry, Earl of Richmond, who then became king as Henry VII. In 1497 King Henry was threatened by a rebellion led by Perkin Warbeck, pretending to be a Yorkist prince, who unsuccessfully besieged the city of Exeter. The city withstood another siege during the rebellion of 1549.

The castle gaol was notorious as a place where prisoners died of starvation and disease was rife. During the Lent Assizes of 1585 Judge Flowerby, eleven jurymen and five magistrates died from a fever said to have spread from the gaol. In Charles I's reign Rougemont Castle was described as an "old ruyning castle whose gaping chinks and aged countenance presageth a downfall ere long". In 1643 the city was captured by the Royalists after an eleven week siege. It was blockaded by a Parliamentary army throughout the winter of 1645-6 but surrendered before Fairfax could storm it. The walls of the castle inner ward seem to have survived intact through this period and most of the them still survive in a much altered state apart from a wide breach on the NW side and a smaller gap east of the Norman gatehouse. The medieval domestic buildings inside were swept away in 1773 and replaced by the Devon Assize Hall and Sessions House, still in use as the county court.

In 1290 Bishop Peter Quinel was licensed by Edward I to embattle the wall of the cathedral close which his palace which adjoined it. The cathedral is now surrounded by houses rather than embattled walls. The palace was mostly rebuilt in 1848, but it has a 14th century gatehouse, a 13th century arch in the SE tower, a 15th century tower porch and a 15m wide hall, originally presumably divided into a nave and aisles.

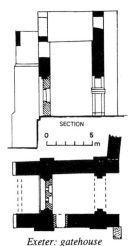

SECTION
0 5 m

Exeter: gatehouse

City walls, Exeter

Although they are not as dramatic or as well maintained as those of York or Chester. the walls of Exeter are amongst the most complete of any English medieval city. They are a 12th and 13th century rebuilding of Roman work with late 14th century repairs. The walls enclose a roughly rectangular area 800m long by 500m wide with the east angle somewhat cambered off and the castle inner ward occupying the north corner, which although the most elevated part of the circuit is the section most exposed to attack. The four main gates have all been destroyed and there is a wide breach in the SW wall south of All Hallows churchyard in the west corner. This SW side has a mill leat cutting off a bow-shaped section of the River Exe, and acting as a moat below the walls. There is also a gap on the NE side. Otherwise something remains of the rest of the circuit, however much altered, damaged or repaired, and most of it can be seen at fairly close range by the public. There are two half-round towers of mid or late 13th century date about 80m apart from each other on the SE side. The northern of these contained two chambers over a vaulted basement. It gained its Lollards Tower from having been used as an ecclesiastical prison by the bishops.

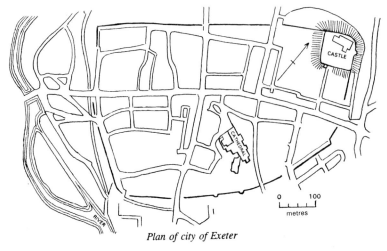

Plan of city of Exeter

GIDLEIGH   SX 670884

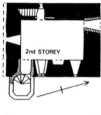

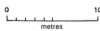

0   10

metres

Plans of Gidleigh Castle

Sir William Prouse, who died in 1316, is thought to have built this small tower. It later belonged to the Coades and the Ridleys and probably had a hall and other outbuildings but these have vanished, leaving the ruined tower as a garden ornament in the grounds of a much later house. The tower is 10.6m long by 7.8m wide and has walls 2m thick in the rib-vaulted basement, reducing to 1.8m at the private room above. There were never any other further storeys and the building only looks one storey high on the west because the land rises rapidly against it. The entrance lies in the south end wall and leads straight into a rib-vaulted cellar with a single loop in the east wall. A staircase from the entrance leads up in two straight flights to a doorway with a draw-bar slot giving onto the private room. This level has a south loop commanding the entrance and on the east is a fireplace with a loop on one side and a bigger embrasure with seats and a two-light window on the other. The doorway at the north end may be a later insertion, probably to a destroyed latrine. Certainly later is the polygonal turret added against the south end of the east wall. This contains a doorway at ground level with a draw-bar slot giving onto a spiral staircase up to a new entrance doorway in the SE corner of the private room.

Gidleigh Castle

Gidleigh Castle

GOMMEROCK   SX 889505

This ruin lies almost opposite Dartmouth Castle close to Kingswear Castle. It could be the lodging which John Corp was licensed to crenellate in 1402 (see page 56) and is mentioned in deeds of 1580 and 1590 as "the old castelle of Kingswear". It measures 11m by 8m and has a ditch dividing it from the high ground, this end only having a parapet. The building may have been a ruin since being damaged in 1643.

GREAT TORRINGTON   SS 497189

A walled late 19th century bowling green above the north side of the River Torridge marks the site of the bailey of this castle. West of it are remains of what may have been a motte. It was probably here in 1139 that Henry de Tracy, a supporter of King Stephen, captured William Fitz-Odo in a surprise attack whilst some of his garrison were out on a raid. The attackers managed to set the main tower alight by throwing torches in through the loopholes. The castle is assumed to have been repaired afterwards. Further strengthening of this site without royal consent in 1228 led to the sheriff of Devon being ordered to demolish the castle and fill in its ditches. Richard Merton was licensed by Edward III to crenellate his dwelling here in 1340, his family having obtained part of the estate by marriage back in 1227. After his death in in 1343, when the castle was given in dower to his widow, there is mention of chambers, a hall, a chapel, a kitchen, a grange and a cowshed. The chapel was dedicated to St James and is mentioned in the 13th century. It was all that remained of the castle when Leland paid a visit c1540. The chapel was later converted into a school but was demolished in 1780. Excavations prior to the construction of a new pavilion at the east end of the site in the 1980s revealed a section of clay-and-stone rampart and foundations of a wall 1m thick with a projection at the south end.

The gateway at Hemyock Castle

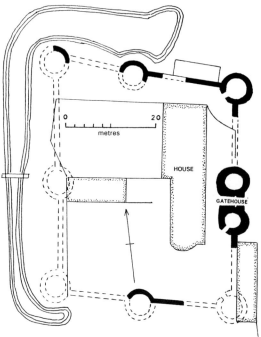

Plan of Hemyock Castle

HEMYOCK   ST 134133

Hemyock was once the seat of the Hidon family and later passed by marriage to the Dynhams. In 1380 Richard II licensed Sir William Asthorpe and his wife Margaret Dynham to crenellate their manor house here. Her family retained possession when Sir William died in 1399. By the 17th century the castle had passed to the Pophams by whom it was garrisoned for Parliament and used to incarcerate Royalists, the Reverend James Burnard being amongst those kept prisoner here. In March 1644 it was besieged by the Royalists but held out until Essex and Waller arrived with a Parliamentary army. Charles II ordered the defences to be slighted after his restoration in 1660. The manor house became a farm, which was sold off without the farmland in the early 1970s.

The castle lies immediately west of the church. A stream between the two buildings fed a wet moat, now drained except around the NW corner. A gateway with a portcullis groove and flanked by the remains of two circular towers survives in the middle of the east side. Only shapeless fragments remain of the towers at the northern corners and in the middle of the south and north sides, whilst hardly anything remains of the curtain wall, and nothing at all of the southern corner towers and another tower assumed to have stood in the middle of the west side. The defences were rather crudely constructed and surrounded a court about 45m from north to south by 34m east-west. It appears that the towers never contained any habitable rooms, and were mostly thinly walled, so they were effectively just for show. The NW tower retains traces of the rendering and limewash which covered all the walls originally. The manor house lies just within the gateway and is still inhabited. It contains work of several periods. Display cases against the north curtain wall contain pottery shards from the site, some going back to the 12th century.

Hemyock Castle

KINGSWEAR SX 891503

This square tower stands on the east side of the mouth of the River Dart and held the other end of the chain stretched across the river from Dartmouth Castle. The tower was begun in 1491, £40 being spent upon it by Dartmouth Corporation in that year. Work continued slowly for ten years. The tower has gunports similar to those at Dartmouth Castle but was more open to the elements so that the iron guns had to be replaced by ones of brass which did not corrode. By the late 16th century guns had improved to the point where those of Dartmouth alone could cover the estuary. The tower was a ruin by the time of the Civil War but was restored as a summer residence by Charles Seale-Hayne in 1855, being connected by a gallery to another building of that date closeby. The castle now belongs to the Landmark Trust.

0 5 m

Kingswear: plans

Kingswear Castle

The keep of Marisco Castle on Lundy

LUNDY   SS 137442 & 142437   F

In 1964 a mound at Bulls Paradise was excavated and found to have a wall 2.1m thick with a blocked alcove overlying an occupation layer and covered by a cobble spread containing late 12th to early 13th century pottery. This is assumed to be the original stronghold of the Marisco family who held Lundy in the mid 12th century. They refused to surrender the island when Henry II granted it to the Knights Templar and used it as a base for raids against the mainland and attacks upon shipping. Much later, in 1242, William de Marisco was captured and Henry III had him hung, drawn and quartered. The existing ruin above Lametry Bay near the SE corner of the island and dominating the landing point is known as Marisco Castle, but it was built after that family had been dispossessed, the Sheriff of Devon being ordered by Henry III in 1243 to "choose a suitable site for a good tower with a bailey-wall with good lime and stone". An inquision of 1321 refers to the castle as having been recently "destroyed and burnt by the Scots". Lundy continued to be used by pirates at various times during the later medieval period, and Queen Elizabeth threatened to take the island from its then owners, the Grenvilles, because they had failed to prevent pirates using it. Despite this, occasional piracy based on the island continued, and in the Civil War the island was one of the last Royalist strongholds to surrender to Parliament, Thomas Bushell not giving it up until February 1648. Much of the remains of the castle may belong to a rebuilding in this period, from which probably also remain the the batteries further north at Brazen Ward and near North East Point. From 1649 to 1658 Lord Saye and Sele occupied the castle, and in c1750 the castle housed convicts working on improvements to the island for Thomas Benson. A journal of 1787 refers to "offices for farming" being constructed from materials taken from the bailey defences shown by Grose in 1775 as fairly intact. Irish labourers housed in the castle in the early 19th century removed all the old woodwork.

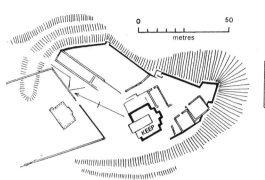

Plan of Marisco Castle, Lundy

Plan of keep of Marisco Castle, Lundy

The keep is a confusing and much altered structure into which fishermen's cottages were built in the mid 19th century, whilst another adjoins the north wall. Since the plan used here was made and the photograph taken these cottages have been restored by the Landmark Trust as four holiday apartments. When the three internal cottages were built the interior was stripped to the bedrock leaving no medieval traces for excavators to find. The outer walls are only 1m thick and may be no older than the 17th century in their present form, the external dimensions being 16.4m by 11.7m. No original cross-wall remains but one would surely have been required to help support an upper floor and the roof. Since the outer wall lacks openings the present layout with windows opening onto a central court may represent the 17th century layout, and possibly even the 13th century one. The east side is stepped out with walling which resembles the rest. There is a parapet with tiny round 18th century corner lookouts not projecting over the walls. The keep lies within a pear-shaped court 85m by 55m with steep drops away from the south and east sides. A thin breastwork partly medieval but mostly 17th century remains on the east with one NE angle turret, a small tower further south, and an angular bastion at the SE corner. A ditch survives on the north but has been filled in on the NW side.

The ringwork at Lydford

LYDFORD   SX 510848   F

Lydford lies on a promontory above the River Lyd and a tributary. It was one of the four boroughs in Devon during the Saxon period and was defended by a stone revetted bank on the weak NE side and more rudimentary defences on the other stronger sides. The forty houses noted in Domesday as having been laid waste may be evidence of castle building. At the tip of the promontory west of the church is a platform about 30m across with a ditch to the east and north. Excavations showed that the bank had been thrown up over early 12th century pottery and that four huts of timber and wickerwork occupied the eastern part of the site, which was later burnt. A coin from King Stephen's reign was amongst the finds. The relationship between this earthwork and the other site north of the church is uncertain.

The other site has what at first appears to be a two storey keep standing on a motte at the SE end of a wedge-shaped bailey 70m long and up to 50m wide with ramparts on the two longest sides and a natural slope on the fourth side. The ramparts are 2m high above the inside but rise up to 7m above the ditches. The keep was generally considered to be the strong building for the keeping of those who broke the laws of the tin miners of Dartmoor erected at Lydford at a cost of £74 on the orders of Richard I in 1195. It was garrisoned in 1198-9 and repaired by King John in 1208 and later seems to have been granted to Richard, Earl of Cornwall. The keep was maintained to serve its original function of courthouse and prison throughout the medieval period. Here in 1510 was incarcerated the Plympton M.P. Richard Strode, who fell foul of the Stannary Court after introducing a bill to curb the Dartmoor miners from clogging up local harbours by their waste. The keep was still in use during the Civil War, the Parliamentarian Colonel James Hals being kept here in 1644 by the Royalists. It was in a poor condition by 1650 and was roofless by 1703, although the judge's chair was then still in position in the courtroom.

The keep at Lydford

The keep measures 14.6m by 14.8m over walls 2.3m thick rising 10m above the external ground level. An entrance with deep draw-bar slots on the NW side leads through to a large room on the SW side of the building. A crosswall divided off two smaller chambers at this level on the NE side. The door of the northern of these two rooms, lighted only by a narrow slit, could be barred against it so it was clearly a prison. The smaller room has an opening in each outer wall of unusual type, being splayed to the outside, although not as much as to the inside. A third opening of this type lights the main room, whose only other feature is a latrine in the west corner. Steps up from the entrance passage lead up to the top storey, also divided by a crosswall, but without the other division, so there were just two rooms. The larger of the two was a hall or courtroom with a latrine in the west corner, a fireplace in the crosswall, and windows facing SE and SW, the latter having seats in the embrasure. A stair from the other embrasure leads to the wall-walk, now lacking its parapet. The other room was a private chamber with three windows and a latrine in the northern corner.

No other Norman keep in England has any loops quite like those of the keep at Lydford and excavations some years ago proved that the history of what had long been assumed to be a late 12th century building of provincial design was actually more complicated. It was discovered that a basement existed, making the building actually 14m high inside. The basement was divided in two had two loops facing SE and one facing NW, clearly indicating that the supposed motte was in fact earth added later against the keep outer face. The walls are here 3m thick and extend beyond the upper walls as a step on the SW side. This basement is clearly older than the superstructure. It could be of 1195 although the sum then spent would not have been sufficient to complete such a massive building, for which a date of c1140-75 seems more likely. The original keep must have been either destroyed or left incomplete and in the 13th century a mound was created over and around the basement which was then filled in except for a small pit. A new prison-cum-courthouse was then raised on top using the old walls as a secure foundation.

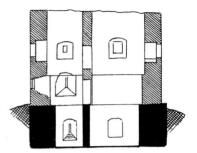

0   10

metres

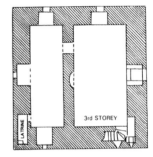

3rd STOREY

LATRINE

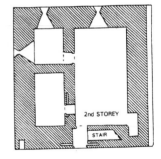

2nd STOREY

STAIR

1st STOREY

Lydford: plans and section of the keep

Interior of the keep at Lydford

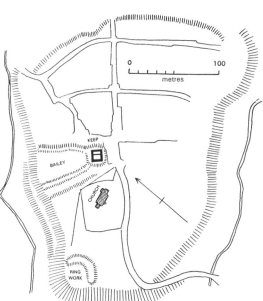

Site plan of Lydford

The keep at Okehampton Castle

The keep at Okehampton Castle

11th Cent
14th Cent
Later

0   10
metres

KEEP

0   3
metres

2nd STOREY

GATE HOUSE

HALL

LATRINES

LATRINE

CHAPEL ABOVE

KITCHENS

KEEP

Plans of Okehampton Castle

OKEHAMPTON   SX 584943

Baldwin Fitz Gilbert, Sheriff of Devon under William I, erected this castle on a spur above the West Okement River, and it is mentioned in Domesday. In 1172 his great-great grandaughter married Robert de Courtenay, who thus came into possession. In 1292 Hugh de Courtenay became Earl of Devon by right of his wife, an heiress of the de Redvers family, and the castle, which had been described in 1273 as "nothing but an old motte" was rebuilt in stone after he obtained his majority in 1297. The Courtenays played a major part in the Wars of the Roses of the 15th century, mostly as Lancastrians. Earl Thomas was executed and attainted by Edward IV in 1461 but the family was restored to power when Henry VII came to the throne. Earl Edward defended Exeter against Perkin Warbeck in 1497 but a few years later he was forfeited. However Henry VIII restored the family to their estates and honours and in 1525 made Edward's grandson Henry the Marquis of Exeter. He supported the king through many controversial policies but in 1537 was implicated in a plot by the Pole family and was executed at the beginning of 1538. His castle at Okehampton was ordered to be dismantled. The only evidence of subsequent occupation is a lease of 1682 allowing John Ellacot, later Mayor of the town, to use the gatehouse and other rooms for a bakehouse. By 1734, when engraved by the Buck brothers, the castle was a ruin looking much as it does now. In the late 19th century Sydney Simmons bought the ruin and in 1917 he handed it over to a trust formed to maintain it. In 1967 it was handed over into the care of the State.

The south side of the bailey at Okehampton Castle

The castle consists of a rectangular mound with a bailey extending down the ridge NE of it. The motte summit measures about 30m long by 20m wide. Upon it is a double tower, a block 10.4m long by 9m wide having been added c1300-20 to a two storey keep 10.4m square with walls about 2m thick probably of c1080-1100. The basement of the later part has a loop in each of the north, west and south walls, and a doorway at the north end of the east wall. The upper storey has a similar layout but with the added features of a fireplace in the south wall and a latrine in the SW corner. The earlier part is more ruinous. It was remodelled and heightened and given a spiral stair in the NE corner beside an entrance at ground level. The lower room had two loops and the upper room had three loops plus a latrine in the SW corner.

Gateway area at Okehampton Castle

The bailey platform has a maximum width of 50m but the stone walls and buildings enclose a rather smaller area. Indeed for the chief seat of an earl the castle has a rather congested plan with the main court no more than 13m wide between the ranges of buildings on each side. The bailey is entered by a square gatehouse at the NE end. The passage was covered by a vault, the ribs of which have been torn out leaving grooves in the walls. A narrow barbican extended down the end of the ridge for 35m to a square outer gateway set awkwardly towards it. East of the gatehouse is the smallest of a series of three lodgings on the SE side of the court. This northern lodging has a latrine beside the gatehouse and the other two have latrines in a projection from the outer wall, here just 1.1m thick. South of the lodgings is the chapel with a piscina and two light windows with trefoil heads on the north and cinquefoil heads on the south. Beyond is a later medieval building provided with an oven in connection with the bakery established here in the 1680s, south of which is a rather more massive section of curtain walling containing a latrine.

A doorway in the gatehouse NW wall leads into an irregularly shaped ante-room from which was reached the hall which is 15m long by 8.5m wide and had a central hearth. A stair in the hall west corner led up to a private room, possibly a solar, though modest in size. The rest of this NW range bends round in the middle and contains a kitchen and other service rooms, one of which has a well, clustered round a small court with a passage through to the hall. Parallel with the kitchen outer wall is a thick length of 14th century curtain walling. Originally this adjoined a thicker and earlier curtain extending round past the hall to meet up with the gatehouse.

Chapel range at Okehampton

PLYMOUTH   SX 484538   V

On the Barbican at the bottom of Lambhay Hill is a small round turret 3m high which is the last remaining part of the fortress called Castle Quadrate. Leland said of Plymouth in 1535 "On the south side of this mouth is a Blok House and on a Rocky Hill hard by is a stronge Castel Quadrante, having at eche corner a great Roundtower. It semith to be no very old Peace of Worke". Despite Leland's last comment this castle may have been founded in the 13th century. Most of the rest of the castle was quarried away long ago. Excavations in the filled-in quarry prior to the site having houses built upon it found many 17th century objects. A rock-cut ditch 6m wide and 3m deep running east-west was discovered and filled in. The remaining turret is said to have been one of a pair flanking the outer gateway. In 1585-8 £132 was spent on works including "filling the barbecon with rubbell and earthe" and "cuveringe of the northe weste tower" and there is mention of Ralph Richards "who stole the leade from the castell", although whether from the roof or from a store is unclear.

Plymouth was a fortified town in the medieval period, a licence to crenellate its walls being granted to the burgesses by Henry IV in 1404. Just to the south of the castle site is the citadel begun in 1666 by Charles II on the site of a fort built in 1592. It has five angle bastions and two horn-works, other outworks having been levelled. The Baroque entrance portal is dated 1670 and is thought to have been designed by Sir Thomas Fitz. Other original buildings are the guard house, the governor's house, doubled in length shortly after completion and rebuilt in 1903, a storehouse and the doorway of the chapel. In the middle of the courtyard is a statue of 1728 of George II with his arm pointing forwards.

At SX 460533, Devil's Point, commanding the mouth of the Hamoaze is a polygonal blockhouse with twin rectangular gunports facing SW and a blocked single one facing south. The ground east of it has risen to such a degree as to block the doorway on the NE side, only its late-medieval type pointed head being visible. This blockhouse has been later adapted as a pillbox and has lost whatever superstructure or parapets it may once have had. There is a much altered seven-sided blockhouse at 464535 and another blockhouse lay at 481536 on the shore below the citadel.

At SX 485533 on the Mount Batten peninsular is a round artillery tower of the 1650s similar to Cromwell's Castle on Tresco, Scilly Isles.

The last remains of Plymouth Castle   *Devil's Point Blockhouse, Plymouth*

The shell keep at Plympton Castle

PLYMPTON   SX 546559   F

This castle was built by Richard de Redvers, Earl of Devon in the late 11th century possibly encorporating earthworks of an older camp above the south side of the Tory Brook. It has a 14m high mound, still with water in the ditch on the north side, and a quadrangular bailey 70m wide extending for 100m to the west. The bailey has a rampart but no ditch survives, nor are there any traces of later curtain walls or buildings. Richard's son Baldwin son rebelled against King Stephen in 1136, and the castle at Plympton was captured and destroyed. The shell keep was possibly built by Baldwin after the Empress Matilda created him Earl of Devon in 1141. About two thirds of the circuit of a shell wall 3m thick enclosing a court 15m in diameter still survives in a fragmentary state to a height of about 4m. A 16th century drawing of the castle suggests there was a round tower within the shell wall, whilst a 14th century illustration shows the bailey with a gateway on the north and a round tower facing west, the evidence for the nature of the keep upper parts being ambiguous. It has been suggested that the inner tower may have been the work of the mercenary captain Fawkes de Breaute, who held Plympton from 1218 to 1224, and thus earlier than the similar arrangement at Launceston. Leland in 1539 described the castle at Plympton as "utterly decayed" but the bailey was occupied by Prince Maurice during the Civil War. No attempt was made to defend the place when a Parliamentary army came to the aid of besieged Plymouth and whatever was habitable was wrecked. The bailey or castle green was later used for sports and fairs. It then belonged to the Earls of Morley, one of whom was forced by the townsfolk to abandon an attempt to plough the site and use it for agriculture. The site is now a public open space.

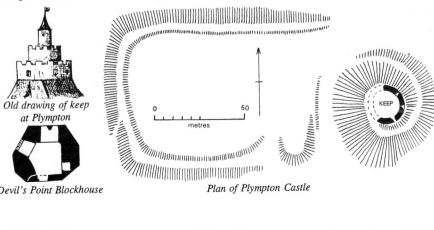

Old drawing of keep at Plympton

Devil's Point Blockhouse

Plan of Plympton Castle

POWDERHAM   SX 968836   O

Domesday Book records Powderham as being held in 1086 by William of Eu, blinded and castrated by William Rufus for rebellion ten years later. In 1150s Reginald de Courtenay obtained the estate by marrying Hawise de Brionne. This family inherited the earldom of Devon from their kinsmen the de Redvers in 1335. The second Earl gave Powderham to his son Sir Philip Courtenay c1390 and the present castle was erected before his death in 1406. In 1553 Queen Mary realeased Edward Courtenay from imprisonment and restored the earldom and estates forfeited by his father on his execution in 1537. He died of poison in 1556 in Italy, having gone into exile on suspicion of involvement in Wyatt's rebellion. The family then lived at Powderham since their original main seat at Okehampton had been adandoned. In 1831 a clerk related to the 3rd Viscount Powderham happened to notice that Queen Mary's letters patent of the earldom given to Edward omitted the usual clause "of his body", thus allowing a more distant relative to inherit the title. Powderham was held by

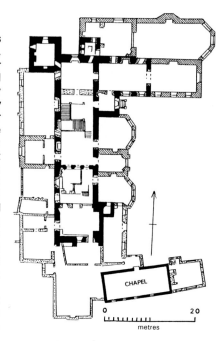

Plan of Powderham Castle

the Royalists under Sir Hugh Meredith against Fairfax during his campaigns in Devon in 1645 but eventually surrendered in 1646 on honourable terms. The castle seems to have been damaged by the siege but was not slighted, perhaps because the Parliamentarian Sir William Waller's daughter was married to the Courtenays.

Powerham Castle from the east

Powderham Castle from the south-west

The castle lies on the end of a low ridge between the River Exe and the River Kenn. The building was a stronghouse or fortified manor house rather than a major fortress but may have been more defensible when the rivers came much closer to the east and south walls, as was the case until the late 18th century. It consisted of a three storey block 39m long and mostly about 9m wide containing a hall with chambers at each end. This shielded the more approachable side of a court about 35m square, now gone, but which the Buck brothers engraving of 1734 shows as having a low embattled wall with a two storey embattled square gatehouse in the middle of the east side, facing out to the sea, and necessitating an approach below the walls on the south side. Boldly projecting from the NW corner of the main block is an original tower about 7m square. The library wing projecting from the north end of the east side also incorporates medieval work. This wing originally contained a chapel but was lengthened and given an addition on the north side beyond a staircase turret in c1710-27, and a bow-ended music room was created in the NW re-entrance angle between these later parts c1795. The towers set not quite opposite each other in the middle of the sides of the main block have been rebuilt in brick but existed by 1734 and may be of medieval origin. Between them lies the Marble Hall on the site of the medieval screens passage, with the usual triple service doorway arrangement south of it, although the openings have been refaced. North of the Marble hall is a wide staircase inserted into the dais end of the medieval hall in the 1750s. The south end of the block is wider, extending further east and having a stair turret at the NE corner. This part may again be a later medieval or 16th century addition. Flanking the central tower on the east side are single storey bow-fronted additions of the 1760s, the northern of which contains the White Drawing Room. The western tower contains a porch. In the 1840s the 10th earl employed Charles Fowler to add banqueting hall north of this porch plus an outer court on this side with its own square gatehouse. On the south side is a 15th century grange converted into a chapel in the 1850s. This thinly walled block, which had been extended eastwards by 1734, was then joined to the main block by extensions.

Salcome Castle

Plan of Tiverton Castle

SALCOME   SX 734381   V

On a rock by the shore, cut off by water at high tide, are remains of a fort built by Henry VIII in the 1540s. On the north, facing the mainland cliff edge, is a ruined wall with the northern half of a round tower or bastion over 10m in diameter to the west and a very ruined polygonal flanker to the east. Colonel Fortescue and 63 men held the fort against Parliament for several weeks, finally surrendering in May 1646. The colonel escaped abroad. His descendants still possess the key to the vanished gate.

Salcombe Castle

TIVERTON SS 954130

The castle lies high above the east bank of the River Eve north of the church. It was founded by Baldwin de Redvers, Earl of Devon, supposedly on the instructions of Henry I. His descendants continued to hold the castle until the male line failed in 1262. Avelina, daughter of the heiress Isabella de Redvers died in 1293 and Tiverton than passed to her kinsman Hugh de Courtenay, created Earl of Devon in 1335 by Edward III. In 1495 William Courtenay married Catherine, daughter of Edward IV, and she lived at Tiverton until 1527. Their son Henry was acknowledged heir-apparent by the young Henry VIII and was created Marquis of Devon, only to be executed and forfeited in 1539 for plotting against the king. The castle and the earldom of Devon then passed to the Duke of Somerset. The estate and title briefly reverted to Edward Courtenay when Mary was on the throne but he died in exile in Padua, the last of his line. By 1588 Tiverton had passed to Roger Giffard. As a result of marrying three wealthy widows in rapid succession he acquired the funds to rebuild parts of the domestic buildings. The Giffards held the castle for King Charles in the Civil War but only managed to put up a token resistance against Fairfax in 1646. He slighted it by demolishing the west and north curtain walls. The castle then passed to the wool merchant Peter West, who erected a new NE wing. He was succeeded by his daughter Dorothy, married to Sir Thomas Carew. Their descendants lived in the castle until it was sold in 1906. A restoration was carried out under the Campbells in the 1960s, but the castle has since passed to their kinsmen the Gordons.

The south side of Tiverton Castle

The SE tower at Tiverton Castle

The castle has a quadrangular court about 50m across from east to west. The width is uncertain as there is no clear evidence of the position of the former north wall. At the SE corner is a round tower about 6m in diameter with three buttresses, apparently original, towards the field. The mullioned windows of the two upper storeys are of c1590. All three levels have fireplaces and have their own direct means of access from the court, there being no internal stairs. Only fragments remain of a hall about 20m long in the SW corner, but most of the 14th century solar wing projecting from the western half of the hall south side still survives. Further north, above the slope to the river is a tower about 7m wide. The early 14th century east range survives in a much altered state. There are original doorways from the court on either side of a fine rib-vaulted gateway passage. The top windows on this side were inserted by Roger Giffard, a datestone of 1588 with his initials having been moved from above the gateway to a block of c1700 in the NE corner. In the early 19th century extensions were made north of the west end of this new block, and then in the 1870s a parallel wing was added to extend the length of the east front. Projecting in front of the vaulted passageway is a tower about 7m wide containing a wider outer section of rib-vaulted passageway apparently of the same period as the inner section. There is now only one upper storey but the Buck brothers' engraving of 1734 shows it as three storeys high, the upper levels reached by a stair in a yet higher octagonal NW turret and having mullioned windows of 1588. At the summit were corbels for a former projecting parapet which may have been machicolated.

The shell keep at Totnes

TOTNES   SX 800605   E

Totnes was granted by William the Conqueror to Judhael, son of Alured, a Breton who later took his name from his castle here. He also founded a Benedictine priory nearby but in 1088 he lost his estates after supporting Robert Curthose against William Rufus. Roger de Nonant was granted Totnes and when Judhael returned to favour under Henry I he lived in his other castle at Barnstaple. Three generations of Robert de Nonant's descendants held Totnes until in 1196 William de Braose, related to Judhael by a female line, managed to obtain possession. In 1205 his son William was made Lord of Totnes by King John, but in 1208 they fell out and de Braose was forfeited. John had his heir put to death and gave Totnes to Henry, son of the long deceased Reginald, Earl of Cornwall. He in turn was forfeited in 1219 and Henry III returned Totnes to Reginald de Braose. Reginald is thought to have built a shell keep on the motte and a fine hall in the bailey. In 1230 Totnes passed to Eva de Braose, married to William de Cantilupe, a notable landowner in the Welsh Marches. In 1244 there is a record of the feudal obligation of the lord's tenants to garrison the castle when required, there being twenty eight "Knight's fees", each one of which was to provide a man-at-arms when needed. In 1265 the townsfolk obtained a grant of murage for building a town wall but the castle then lay empty and neglected. In 1273 an inquest after the death of the young George de Cantilupe describes the defences and buildings of the bailey as "weak and ruinous" and the keep as partly fallen down.

Interior of the keep at Totnes

Totnes then passed to Millicent de Cantilupe, wife of Eudo de la Zouche. Their son William, created Baron Zouche of Harringworth, rebuilt the castle, having obtained an order from the then captive Edward II for this purpose in 1326. The Zouches never actually lived in the castle but they insisted on the tenants maintaining the keep. In 1343 a tenant unsuccessfully tried to avoid this obligation on the grounds that his lord no longer used the castle. In 1463 and 1471 the tenants were ordered to repair the keep probably in expectation of a Lancastrian resurgence, for the Zouches were ardent Yorkists. After Richard III's defeat at Bosworth Henry VII forfeited John, 6th Lord Zouche of Harringworth and granted Totnes to Sir Richard Edgecombe of Cotehele. The keep was still being maintained when Leland visited Totnes c1535 but the buildings in the bailey were ruinous. Sir Piers Edgecombe sold the castle c1559 to Sir Edward Seymour. The castle took no part in the Civil War and passed to the Bogan family in 1655 but was purchased back by the Seymours in 1764. The Duke of Somerset placed the ruins in State care in 1947.

The castle lies on a hill commanding the upper end of the navigable section of the River Dart. The motte commands the NW end of the town and the bailey extends beyond it, outside of the modest area just 300m long by 160m enclosed by the town walls. Of the 13th century town walls several sections survive with a square gatehouse closing off the east end of High Street and a north gateway which is just a plain lofty semi-circular arch near the castle. Two other gates have gone. The castle bailey measures about 66m across. The 14th century curtain wall only survives around a quarter of the circuit on the west, the other walls being thin, low and more recent. A deep ditch 22m wide protects the northern and western sides, where there is an outer bank. Traces of footings of buildings have been detected in dry weather, and it is thought the hall lay on the west with the chapel at the north end of it.

Bailey walls at Totnes Castle

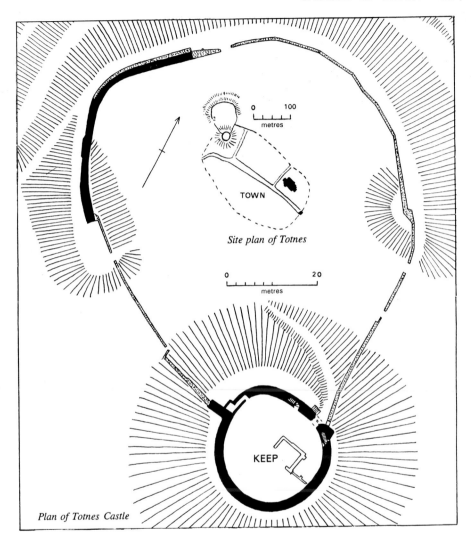

Site plan of Totnes

Plan of Totnes Castle

A path now zig-zags up the motte but the original approach to the keep is thought to have followed the bailey east curtain wall. The existing shell wall is 14th century but may incorporate parts of its 13th century predessessor. The wall is 1.8m thick above a tall battered base and has a wall-walk rising 3.7m above the interior and 5.5m above the outside ground level. The parapet is remarkably complete, owing perhaps to the obligation on the tenants to repair it being long enforced. The shell wall has two stairs to the wall-walk set either side of the entrance on the north, and on the west is a passage to a latrine contained in a thickening of the wall. Corbels remain for the roof of a lean-to building in this section, footings of one end wall also surviving. East of the middle of the court are stone footings which supported a timber tower about 6m by 5m. This feature seems to be as old as the motte and is known to go at least 3.3m down into it, so it was presumably raised at the same time.

WEMBWORTHY   SS 679125 & 678119

On the top of a spur above the west bank of the River Taw, and now buried in undergrowth in woods, is a ringwork 22m in diameter with a rampart rising 3.5m above the interior and up to 7.5m above the surrounding ditch. A horse-shoe shaped bailey 50m by 35m lies to the NE. It has a rampart 2m high rising 4.5m above a ditch. Not far to the east, on the very edge of the drop to the river lies a second ringwork and bailey, both parts being of a rather elongated form from north to south. Neither required man-made defences on the east side. The ringwork lies at the south end measures 40m by 30m. It has a rampart 3.5m high rising 5.5m above the ditch. The bailey measures 80m by 43m and has a rampart on the west and north sides.

WINKLEIGH   SS 631080 & 633082

North of the west end of Castle Street is a mound called Croft Castle which rises 6m to a dished summit 15m across. About 250m to the NE, and probably later in date, is an oval platform about 55m by 45m with a ditch up to 20m wide at the north end.

Entrance and NE tower at Compton Castle

Bayard's Cove Castle, Dartmouth

OTHER MEDIEVAL FORTIFIED SITES IN DEVON

AFFETON BARTON SS 755137 Facing west is an embattled range with a blocked gateway passage. Built by the Affetons in the 15th century and altered by the Stucleys in 1868. Other medieval parts also survive.

BERE FERRERS SX 459634 Ferrers family licenced to crenellate 1337 and 1340.

BOW SX 730740 A platform 25m by 20m rises 4m above dried up bed of moat extending 35m to dam on NE side. Henry de Tracy had a market at Bow in 1259.

BRATTON FLEMING SS 645378 Much damaged motte.

BRIDESTOWE SX 498876 NE of a camp with a rampart and ditch lies a ditched motte with a half-moon shaped bailey 40m by 20m on the NE side.

BUCKLAND ABBEY SX 487668 Licence to crenellate granted by Edward III in 1337.

CHUDLEIGH SX 866789 A licence to crenellate a manor house here or elsewhere was granted by Richard II in 1379 to Thomas Brantingham, Bishop of Exeter.

COLDRIDGE SS 667058 This is a ringwork with a small bailey and an outwork.

EAST STONEHOUSE SX 465546 Licence to crenellate granted to Sir Peter Edgecombe by Henry VIII in 1515.

HATCH SX 710469 Licence to crenellate granted in 1462 to Thomas Gille.

HEMBURY SX 725684 On the west side of ear-shaped hillfort is a ditched motte within a bailey platform 70m long by 50m wide.

HIGHWEEK SX 846719 The small, low motte has a dished summit 12m across. A bailey plarform extends 35m to the SW. An old plan suggests it may have once surrounded the motte.

HOLWELL SS 670446 Above the south side of the River Heddon south of the village of Parracome is a motte and bailey site known as Holwell Castle.

ILTON SX 727405 Licence to crenellate granted in 1335 to John Cheureston.

KENTISBURY SS 623438 Licence to crenellate granted to John Wolf in 1457.

LANGFORD SX 699566 This is a damaged or unfinished motte near Ugborough.

LODDISWELL SX 720520 A ringwork about 25 across with a bailey 50m by 30m defended by a rampart 4m high lies in the NW corner of an Iron Age fort.

LOXORE SS 620377 The mound called Castle Roborough high above the River Yeo rises 4.5m to a summit 12m across with a 2m deep depression in the middle.

MILTON DAMERELL SS 397127 U-shaped platform 42m by 28m with 14m wide ditch above River Torridge. Higher, curved west end may be unfinished motte.

MODBURY SX 656516 Licence to crenellate given to Richard Champernowe, 1334.

NORTH TAWTON SS 666018 Mound called Castle Court 100m east of church rises 3m to summit 16m by 14m. Ditch filled in except on the south side.

NUTWELL SX 997850 Said to have been a stronghouse similar to Powderham.

SAMPFORD PEVERELL ST 028145 Oliver Dinham was licenced to crenellate his house here by Edward III in 1337 and 1339.

SHUTE BARTON SY 254972 The Bonvilles' embattled three storey house of 1380 with gateway adjoining. Later passed to the Greys. The Poles added outer court with gatehouse on acquiring the house in 1570.

STONE BARTON SS 713142 Slight traces of what are said to be footings of stone walled court with gatehouse on promontory above the Little Dart.

TAMERTON SX 470610 Licence to crenellate granted in 1335 to John Ocle.

TEIGNMOUTH The town is said to have had a defensive wall in the 16th century.

WIDWORTHY SY 313995 Low, damaged motte created out of hillock at ridge end.

WYCROFT SY 308998 Licence to crenellate granted in 1427 to Thomas Brooke.

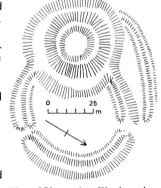

0   25
m

Plan of Ringwork at Wembworthy

GLOSSARY OF TERMS

ASHLAR - Masonry of blocks with even faces and square edges. BAILEY - Defensible court enclosed by a wall or a palisade and ditch. BARBICAN - Defensible court, passage or porch in front of an entrance. BASTION - A projection rising no higher than the curtain wall. BRATTICE - A covered wooden gallery at the summit of a wall for defending its base. CORBEL - A projecting bracket to support other stonework or a timber beam. CURTAIN WALL - A high enclosing stone wall around a bailey. DEMI-BASTION - Bastion flanking just one side of the enciente instead of two. EMBATTLED - Provided with a a parapet with indentations (crenellations). FOUR-CENTRED ARCH - An arch drawn with four compass points, two on each side. GUNPORT -an embrasure suitable for the discharge of heavy cannon. JAMB - A side of a doorway, window or other opening. KEEP - A citadel or ultimate strongpoint. The term is not medieval and such towers were then called donjons, from which word is derived the word dungeon meaning a prison. LIGHT - A compartment of a window. LOOP - A small opening to admit light or for the discharge of missiles. MACHICOLATION - A slot for dropping or firing missiles at assailants. MANTLET - A low wall or parapet enclosing a narrow space in front of a tower or curtain wall. MERLONS - The upstanding portions of a parapet. MOAT - A defensive ditch, water filled or dry. MOTTE - A steep sided flat-topped mound, partly or wholly man-made. OILLET - Small circular hole. PARAPET - A wall for protection at any sudden drop. PLINTH - The projecting base of a wall. It may be battered (sloped) or stepped. PORTCULLIS - A wooden gate made to rise and fall in vertical grooves, being hoisted by a windlass above. POSTERN - A back entrance or lesser gateway. RINGWORK - An embanked enclosure of more modest size than a bailey, generally of greater width but less elevated than a motte summit. SHELL KEEP - A small stone walled court built upon a motte or ringwork. SOLAR - A private living room for the lord and his family. TOWER HOUSE - Self contained defensible house with the main rooms stacked vertically. WALL-WALK - A walkway on top of a wall, always protected by a parapet. WARD - A stone walled defensive enclosure.

PUBLIC ACCESS TO THE SITES   Codes used in the gazetteers.

E Buildings in the care of English Heritage. Fee payable at some sites.
F Sites to which there is free access at any time.
H Buildings currently used as hotels, restaurants, shops (free access to outside).
O Buildings opened to the public by private owners, local councils, National Trust.
V Buildings closely visible from public roads, paths, churchyards & open spaces.

FURTHER READING

The Buildings of Cornwall, Nikolaus Pevsner, Buildings of England Series, 1952.
The Buildings of Devon, Bridget Cherry & Nikolaus Pevsner, as above, 1952 & 1989
The Victoria Country History of Devon
Discovering Devonsire castles and forts, Colin Pomeroy
English Heritage has pamphlets available for Berry Pomeroy, Dartmouth, Launceston, Okehampton, Pendennis, Restormel, St Mawes, Scilly Isles forts, Tintagel, Totnes
Pamphlets or leaflets are are available for Carn Brea, Compton, Hemyock, Lundy, Pengersick, Powderham, St Michael's Mount.
See also articles on Bickleigh and Powderham in Country Life. Other useful articles occur in the Archeological Journal and Medieval Archeology.